Fodor's® New

FIRST EDITION

Pocket
Amsterdam

Excerpted from Fodor's *The Netherlands, Belgium, Luxembourg*

Fodor's Travel Publications, Inc.
New York • Toronto • London • Sydney • Auckland
www.fodors.com

Fodor's Pocket Amsterdam

EDITORS: Lauren A. Myers, Nancy van Itallie

Editorial Contributors: David Brown, Linda Burnham, Brent Gregston, Andrew May, Helayne Schiff

Editorial Production: Linda K. Schmidt

Maps: David Lindroth, *cartographer*; Steven Amsterdam and Bob Blake, *map editors*

Design: Fabrizio La Rocca, *creative director*; Guido Caroti, *associate art director*; Lyndell Brookhouse-Gil, *cover design*; Jolie Novak, *photo editor*

Production/Manufacturing: Mike Costa

Cover Photograph: G. Anderson/The Stock Market

Copyright

First Edition

ISBN 0–679–00243–X

Special Sales

PRINTED IN THE UNITED STATES OF AMERICA

10 9 8 7 6 5 4 3 2 1

CONTENTS

Maps

ON THE ROAD WITH FODOR'S

WHEN I PLAN a vacation, the first thing I do is cast around among my friends and colleagues to find someone who's just been where I'm going. That's because there's no substitute for a recommendation from a good friend who knows your tastes, your budget, and your circumstances, someone who's just been there. Unfortunately, such friends are few and far between. So it's nice to know that there's *Fodor's Pocket Amsterdam*.

In the first place, this book won't stay home when you hit the road. It will accompany you every step of the way, steering you away from wrong turns and wrong choices and never expecting a thing in return. Most important of all, it's written and assiduously updated by the kind of people you *would* hit up for travel tips if you knew them. They're as choosy as your pickiest friend, except they've probably seen a lot more of Amsterdam. In these pages, they don't send you chasing down every town and sight in town but have instead selected the best ones, the ones that are worthy of your time and money.

About Our Writers

Our success in helping to make your trip the best of all possible vacations is a credit to the hard work of our extraordinary writers and editors.

Linda Burnham, who wrote the bulk of this book, began her love affair with Amsterdam—and travel—perched on a settee in the lobby of the Amstel Hotel at the beginning of a post-college Eurorail tour. Six years on staff with KLM later turned Holland into more than a destination: It became a second home. Her Dutch friends say she knows their country better than they do. She has co-authored several books about the Netherlands, the Caribbean, and the United States, and has written for *Travel & Leisure, Harper's Bazaar, Modern Bride,* and *Condé Nast Traveler.*

Brent Gregston lives in Amsterdam. After studying philosophy in Freiburg, Germany, he worked as a translator for the U.S. State Department and later as an editor for an on-line travel site.

Andrew May was born and raised in northeast England. At first he put his training in violin, piano, musicology, and marketing to work as a classical music reviewer. Moving to Amsterdam in 1992, he diversified into translation, wrote his own travel guide, and started contributing to Fodor's guidebooks. Despite an unshakeable British accent when using their language, he hopes never to cease surprising the Dutch with more knowledge of the Netherlands than they usually expect to amass in a lifetime.

Connections

We're pleased that the American Society of Travel Agents continues to endorse Fodor's as its guidebook of choice. ASTA is the world's largest and most influential travel trade association, operating in more than 170 countries, with 27,000 members pledged to adhere to a strict code of ethics reflecting the Society's motto, "Integrity in Travel." ASTA shares Fodor's devotion to providing smart, honest travel information and advice to travelers, and we've long recommended that our readers—even those who have guidebooks and traveling friends—consult ASTA member agents for the experience and professionalism they bring to your vacation planning.

On Fodor's Web site (www. fodors.com), check out the new Resource Center, an on-line companion to the Gold Guide section of this book, complete with useful hot links to related sites. In our forums, you can also get lively advice from other travelers and more great tips from Fodor's experts worldwide.

How to Use This Book

Organization

Up front is **Essential Information,** an easy-to-use section arranged alphabetically by topic. Under each listing you'll find tips and information that will help you accomplish what you need to in Amsterdam. You'll also find addresses and telephone numbers of organizations and companies that offer destination-related services and information.

The first chapter, Destination: Amsterdam, helps get you in the mood for your trip. Quick Tours lays out a selection of half-day itineraries that will help you make the most of your time in Amsterdam.

The **Exploring Amsterdam** chapter is divided into three neighborhoods. Each lists sights alphabetically and has a suggested walk which will take you around to the major sights.

The remaining chapters are arranged in alphabetical order by subject—**Dining, Lodging, Nightlife and the Arts, Shopping, and Side Trips from Amsterdam.**

Icons and Symbols

★   Our special recommendations

✕   Restaurant

🏠   Lodging establishment

👆   Good for kids (rubber duck)

☞   Sends you to another section of the guide for more information

✉   Address

☎   Telephone number

🕐   Opening and closing times

💷   Admission prices (those we give apply only to adults; substantially reduced fees are almost always available for children, students, and senior citizens)

Numbers in white and black circles (e.g., ③ ❸) that appear on the maps, in the margins, and within the tours correspond to one another.

Dining and Lodging

The restaurants and lodgings we list are the cream of the crop in each price range. Price charts appear at the beginning of Chapters 3 and 4.

Hotel Facilities

We always list the facilities that are available—but we don't specify whether they cost extra: When pricing accommodations, always ask what's included. Assume that hotels operate on the **European Plan** (EP, with no meals).

Restaurant Reservations and Dress Codes

Reservations are always a good idea; we note only when they're essential or when they are not accepted. Book as far ahead as you can, and reconfirm as soon as you arrive. Unless otherwise noted, the restaurants listed are open daily for lunch and dinner. We mention dress only when men are required to wear a jacket or a jacket and tie.

Credit Cards

The following abbreviations are used: **AE**, American Express; **DC**, Diners Club; **MC**, MasterCard; and **V**, Visa.

Don't Forget to Write

You can use this book in the confidence that all prices and opening times are based on information supplied to us at press time; Fodor's cannot accept responsibility for any errors. Time inevitably brings changes, so always confirm information when it matters—especially if you're making a detour to visit a specific place.

Were the restaurants we recommended as described? Did our hotel picks exceed your expectations? Did you find a museum we recommended a waste of time? Keeping a travel guide fresh and up-to-date is a big job, and we welcome your feedback, positive *and* negative. If you have complaints, we'll look into them and revise our entries when the facts warrant it. If you've discovered a special place that we haven't included, we'll pass the information along to our correspondents and have them check it out. So send your thoughts via e-mail at editors@fodors.com (specifying the name of the book on the subject line) or on paper in care of the Pocket Amsterdam editor at Fodor's, 201 East 50th Street, New York, New York 10022. In the meantime, have a wonderful trip!

Karen Cure

Karen Cure
Editorial Director

The Netherlands

North Sea

Schiermonnikoog
Delfzijl
Ameland
Groningen
Winschoten
Terschelling
Dokkum
Leeuwarden
Drachten
Assen
Vlieland
Harlingen
Emmen
Bolsward
Texel
Sneek
Hoogeveen
Waddenzee
Meppel
Den Helder
IJsselmeer
Zwolle
Almelo
Hengelo
Enkhuizen
Alkmaar
Lelystad
Hoorn
Deventer
Enschede
Zaanstad
Purmerend
Apeldoorn
Amsterdam
Haarlem
Bussum
Winterswijk
Hilversum
Amersfoort
Arnhem
Doetinchem
Leiden
Utrecht
Oude Rijn
Neder Rijn
Den Haag
(The Hague)
Tiel
Nijmegen
Rhine
GERMANY
Delft
Rotterdam
Waal
Oss
Maas
's Hertogenbosch
Dordrecht
Veghel
Haringvliet
Overflakkee
Schouwen/
Duiveland
Steenbergen
Breda
Tilburg
Eindhoven
Tholen
Weert
Goes
Bergen op Zoom
Roermond
Walcheren
Beveland
Middelburg
Westerschelde
Sittard
Breskens
Terneuzen
Antwerp
Maastricht
Aachen
Vaals
BELGIUM
Liège
KEY
Ferry
40 miles
Brussels
60 km
Grevelingen
Oosterschelde
Schelde
N34

Amsterdam

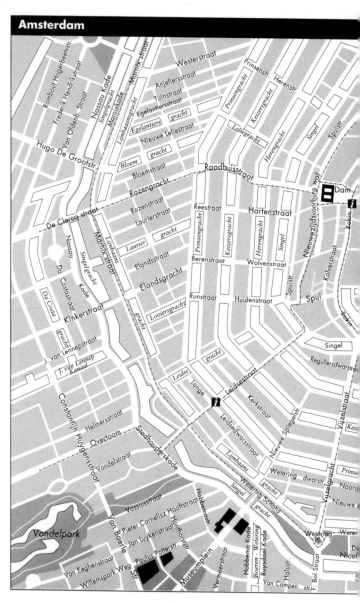

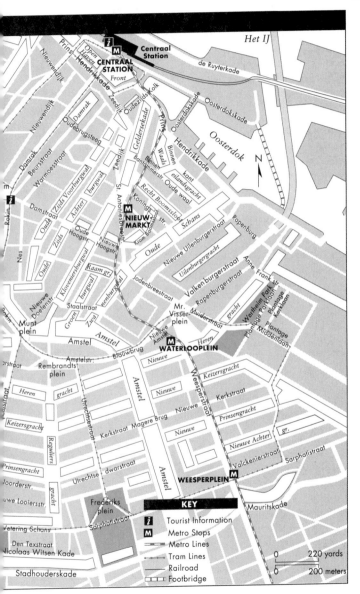

Het IJ

Centraal Station

de Ruyterkade

CENTRAAL STATION

Open Haven Front

Oosterdokskade

Oosterdok

Hendrikkade

N

Prins Hendrikkade

Nieuwendijk

Damrak

Oudebrugsteeg

Gelderskade

Prins

Wads

Binnen Bantammerstr.

kant eilandsgracht

Oude waal

Recht Boomssloot

Koningsstr.

Recht Boomssloot

Schans

Rapenburg

Nieuwendijk

Beurstraat

Warmoesstraat

Zeedijk

St. Antoniesbreestr.

NIEUWMARKT

Krom Boom

Oude

Nieuwe Uilenburgergracht

Anne Frank str.

Damstraat

Zijds Voorburgwal

Achter burgwal

Nieuwe Hoogstr.

Oude Hoogstr.

Uilenburgergracht

Valkenburgerstraat

Rapenburgerstraat

Oude Zijds

Nieuwe Doelenstr.

Klovenierburgwal

Raam gr.

burgwal

venburgwal

Jodenbreestraat

Mr. Visser plein

Muiderstraat

Wertheim Park

Plantage Kerklaan

Nes

Oude

Rokin

Munt plein

Groen

Zwd

Staalstraat

Amstel

Nieuwe Amstel

Heren

Plantage Parklaan

Plantage Middenlaan

Amstel

Rembrandts plein

Amstelstr.

Blaauwbrug

WATERLOOPLEIN

Nieuwe

Keizersgracht

Heren

gracht

Utrechtsestraat

Kerkstraat

Magere Brug

Nieuwe

Nieuwe

Weesperstraat

Kerkstraat

Prinsengracht

Keizersgracht

Reguliers

gracht

Nieuwe

Nieuwe Achter gr.

Prinsengracht

Utrechtse dwarstraat

Amstel

Valckenierstraat

Sarphatistraat

Joorderstr.

uwe Looiersstr.

Frederiks plein

WEESPERPLEIN

Mauritskade

Vetering Schans

Den Texstraat

Nicolaas Witsen Kade

Sarphatistraat

Stadhouderskade

KEY

🛈 Tourist Information

Ⓜ Metro Stops

━━━ Metro Lines

┈┈┈ Tram Lines

━━━ Railroad

▭▭▭ Footbridge

0   220 yards

0   200 meters

ESSENTIAL INFORMATION

*Basic Information on Traveling in Amsterdam,
Savvy Tips to Make Your Trip a Breeze, and
Companies and Organizations to Contact*

AIR TRAVEL

Flying time to Amsterdam from New York is just over seven hours; from Chicago, closer to eight hours; and from Los Angeles, 10½ hours. Flying time to Amsterdam from London is one hour.

BOOKING YOUR FLIGHT

Price is just one factor to consider when booking a flight: frequency of service and even a carrier's safety record are often just as important. Major airlines offer the greatest number of departures. Smaller airlines—including regional and no-frills airlines—usually have a limited number of flights daily. On the other hand, so-called low-cost airlines usually are cheaper, and their fares impose fewer restrictions, such as advance-purchase requirements. Safety-wise, low-cost carriers as a group have a good history—about equal to that of major carriers.

When you book, **look for nonstop flights** and **remember that "direct" flights stop at least once.** Try to **avoid connecting flights,** which require a change of plane. Two airlines may jointly operate a connecting flight, so ask if your airline operates every segment— you may find that your preferred carrier flies you only part of the way. International flights on a country's flag carrier are almost always nonstop; U.S. airlines often fly direct.

Ask your airline if it offers electronic ticketing, which eliminates all paperwork. There's no ticket to pick up or misplace. You go directly to the gate and give the agent your confirmation number instead of waiting in line at the counter while precious minutes tick by.

CARRIERS

When flying internationally, you must usually choose between a domestic carrier, the national flag carrier of the country you are visiting, and a foreign carrier from a third country. National flag carriers have the greatest number of nonstops. Domestic carriers may have better connections to your home town and serve a greater number of gateway cities. Third-party carriers may have a price advantage.

➤ FROM THE U.K.: **Aer Lingus** (☎ 0181/899–4747 in the U.K.), **British Airways** (☎ 0181/897–4000 in the U.K.), and **KLM** (☎ 0990/750–9000 in the U.K.).

➤ MAJOR AIRLINES: **Delta** (☎ 800/221–1212). **Northwest** (☎ 800/225–2525).**TWA** (☎ 800/892–4141). **United** (☎ 800/241–6522).

➤ NATIONAL CARRIERS: **KLM Royal Dutch Airlines** (☎ 800/374–7747 in the U.S.).

➤ REGIONAL CARRIERS: **KLM City Hopper** (☎ 020/474–7747) provides regular service between Amsterdam Schiphol Airport and Rotterdam, Eindhoven, and Maastricht, although air travel in a country this small is really unnecessary.

CHECK IN & BOARDING

Airlines routinely overbook planes, assuming that not everyone with a ticket will show up, but sometimes everyone does. When that happens, airlines ask for volunteers to give up their seats. In return these volunteers usually get a certificate for a free flight and are rebooked on the next flight out. If there are not enough volunteers, the airline must choose who will be denied boarding. The first to be bumped are passengers who checked in late and those flying on discounted tickets, so **get to the gate and check in as early as possible**, especially during peak periods.

Although the trend on international flights is to drop reconfirmation requirements, many airlines still ask you to reconfirm each leg of your international itinerary. Failure to do so may result in your reservations being canceled.

Always **bring a government-issued photo ID to the airport.** You may be asked to show it before you are allowed to check in.

CONSOLIDATORS

Consolidators buy tickets for scheduled international flights at reduced rates from the airlines, then sell them at prices that beat the best fare available directly from the airlines, usually without restrictions. Sometimes you can even get your money back if you need to return the ticket. Carefully read the fine print detailing penalties for changes and cancellations, and **confirm your consolidator reservation with the airline.**

➤ CONSOLIDATORS: **Cheap Tickets** (☎ 800/377–1000). **Discount Travel Network** (☎ 800/576–1600). **Unitravel** (☎ 800/325–2222). **Up & Away Travel** (☎ 212/889–2345). **World Travel Network** (☎ 800/409–6753).

CUTTING COSTS

The least-expensive airfares to the Netherlands are priced for round-trip travel and usually must be purchased in advance. It's smart to **call a number of airlines, and when you are quoted a good price, book it on the spot**—the same fare may not be available the next day. Airlines generally allow you to change your return date for a fee. If you don't use your ticket, you can apply the cost toward the purchase of a new ticket, again for a small charge. However, most low-fare tickets are nonrefundable. To get the lowest airfare, **check different routings.** Compare prices of flights to and from different airports if your destination or home city has more than one gateway. Also price off-peak flights, which may be significantly less expensive.

Travel agents, especially those who specialize in finding the lowest fares (☞ Discounts & Deals, *below*), can be especially helpful when booking a plane ticket. When you're quoted a price, **ask your agent if the price is likely to drop any lower.** Good agents know the seasonal fluctuations of airfares and can usually anticipate a sale or fare war. However, waiting can be risky: The fare could go *up* as seats become scarce, and you may wait so long that your preferred flight sells out. A wait-and-see strategy works best if your plans are flexible. If you must arrive and depart on certain dates, don't delay.

ENJOYING THE FLIGHT

For more legroom, **request an emergency-aisle seat.** Don't sit in the row in front of the emergency aisle or in front of a bulkhead, where seats may not recline.

If you don't like airline food, **ask for special meals when booking.** These can be vegetarian, low-cholesterol, or kosher.

When flying internationally, try to maintain a normal routine, to help fight jet-lag. At night, **get some sleep.** By day, **eat light meals, drink water (not alcohol), and move around the cabin** to stretch your legs.

Many carriers prohibit smoking on all of their international flights; others allow smoking only on certain routes or certain departures, so **contact your carrier regarding its smoking policy.**

HOW TO COMPLAIN

If your baggage goes astray or your flight arrangements go awry, complain right away. Most carriers require that you **file a claim immediately.**

➤ AIRLINE COMPLAINTS: U.S. Department of Transportation **Aviation Consumer Protection Division** (✉ C-75, Room 4107, Washington, DC 20590, ☎ 202/366–2220). **Federal Aviation Administration Consumer Hotline** (☎ 800/322–7873).

AIRPORTS AND CITY TRANSFERS

AIRPORTS

Amsterdam Schiphol Airport is 25 km (15 mi) southeast of the city and has efficient road and rail links. The comprehensive "Helloport" telephone service, charged at Fl 1 per minute, provides information about flight arrivals and departures as well as all transport and parking facilities.

➤ AIRPORT INFORMATION: **Schiphol Airport** (☎ 31/6/350–34050).

CITY TRANSFERS

Between the airport and downtown: KLM Shuttle operates a shuttle bus service between Schiphol Airport and major city hotels. The trip takes about a half hour and costs Fl 17.50 one-way. The Schiphol Rail Link operates between the airport and the city 24 hours a day, with service to the central railway station or to stations in the south of the city. The trip takes about 15 minutes and costs Fl 5.75. There is a taxi stand in front of the arrival hall at Schiphol Airport. All taxis are metered, and the fare is approximately Fl 60 to central Amsterdam. Service is included, but small additional tips are not unwelcome.

➤ CONTACTS: **KLM Shuttle** (☎ 020/649–5651). **Schiphol Rail Link** (☎ 0900/9292).

BIKE TRAVEL

Bicycling is the most convenient way to see Amsterdam. There are bike lanes on all major streets, bike racks in key locations, and special bike parking indentations in the pavement. If you decide to rent a bicycle, expect to pay from Fl 10 per day, plus a deposit of Fl 50–Fl 200 per bike. You'll need a passport or other identification to rent.

➤ BIKE RENTALS: **Centraal Station** (✉ Stationsplein 12, 1012 AB, ☎ 020/624–8391). **McBike**

(✉ Marnixstraat 220, 1016 TL, ☎ 020/626–6964).

BOAT & FERRY TRAVEL

➤ FROM THE U.K.: **Hoverspeed LTD** (☎ 01843/595522) has services between Dover and Oostende with up to eight daily round trips. **P&O North Sea Ferries** (✉ King George Dock, Hedon Rd., Hull HU9 5QA, UK, ☎ 01482/377177) operates overnight ferry services from Hull to Zeebrugge and Rotterdam; the trip takes 3 to 12 hours, depending on the route. **Stena Line** (✉ Charter House, Park St., Ashford, Kent TN24 BEX UK, ☎ 01233/647047) operates hydrofoils and a car ferry service twice daily between Harwich in Essex and Hoek van Holland.

BUS TRAVEL

➤ FROM THE U.K.: **Eurolines** (✉ 4 Cardiff Rd., Luton, Bedfordshire, LU11PP, UK, ☎ 0990/143219 in the U.K.; ☎ 540/298–1395 in U.S.; ☎ 020/560–8787 in the Netherlands) operates Bus/ferry combination service between London and Amsterdam.

CAMERAS & COMPUTERS

EQUIPMENT PRECAUTIONS

Always **keep your film, tape, or computer disks out of the sun.** Carry an extra supply of batteries, and **be prepared to turn on your camera, camcorder, or laptop** to prove to security personnel that the device is real. Always **ask for hand inspection of film,** which becomes clouded after successive exposure to airport X-ray machines, and **keep videotapes and computer disks away from metal detectors.**

➤ PHOTO HELP: **Kodak Information Center** (☎ 800/242–2424). *Kodak Guide to Shooting Great Travel Pictures,* available in bookstores or from Fodor's Travel Publications (☎ 800/533–6478; $16.50 plus $4 shipping).

CAR RENTAL

The major car rental firms have booths at Schiphol Airport. This is convenient, but the airport charges rental companies a fee that is passed on to customers, so you may want to wait until you arrive at the downtown locations of rental firms.

Rates in Amsterdam vary from company to company; daily rates start at approximately $50 for a one-day rental, $140 for a three-day rental, and $190 for a week's rental. This does not include collision insurance, airport fee, or 17.5% VAT tax. Weekly rates often include unlimited mileage.

➤ MAJOR AGENCIES: **Alamo** (☎ 800/522–9696, 0800/272–2000 in the U.K.). **Avis** (☎ 800/331–1084, 800/879–2847 in Canada, 008/225–533 in Australia). **Budget** (☎ 800/527–0700, 0800/181181 in the U.K.). **Dollar** (☎ 800/800–4000; 0990/565656 in the U.K., where it is known as Eurodollar). **Hertz** (☎ 800/654–

3001, 800/263–0600 in Canada, 0345/555888 in the U.K., 03/9222–2523 in Australia, 03/358–6777 in New Zealand). **National InterRent** (☎ 800/227–3876; 0345/222525 in the U.K., where it is known as Europcar InterRent).

➤ IN AMSTERDAM: **Avis** (⊠ Nassaukade 380, ☎ 020/683–6061), **Budget** (⊠ Overtoom 121, ☎ 020/612–6066), and **Hertz** (⊠ Overtoom 333, ☎ 020/612–2441) operate desks at the airport and have rental offices in Amsterdam and other key cities throughout the Netherlands. In addition, the Dutch firm **Van Wijk Amsterdam** (Amsterdam Schiphol Airport, ☎ 020/601–5277) operates at the airport and other locations.

CUTTING COSTS

To get the best deal, **book through a travel agent who is willing to shop around.**

Also **ask your travel agent about a company's customer-service record.** How has the company responded to late plane arrivals and vehicle mishaps? Are there often lines at the rental counter? If you're traveling during a holiday period, does a confirmed reservation guarantee you a car?

Be sure to **look into wholesalers,** companies that do not own fleets but rent in bulk from those that do and often offer better rates than traditional car-rental operations. Prices are best during off-peak periods. Rentals booked through wholesalers must be paid for before you leave the United States.

➤ RENTAL WHOLESALERS: **Auto Europe** (☎ 207/842–2000 or 800/223–5555, FAX 800–235–6321). **DER Travel Services** (☎ 800/782–2424, FAX 800/282–7474 for information or 800/860–9944 for brochures). **Europe by Car** (☎ 212/581–3040 or 800/223–1516, FAX 212/246–1458). **Kemwel Holiday Autos** (☎ 914/835–5555 or 800/678–0678, FAX 914/835–5126).

INSURANCE

When driving a rented car you are generally responsible for any damage to or loss of the vehicle. Before you rent, **see what coverage you already have** under the terms of your personal auto-insurance policy and credit cards.

Collision policies that car-rental companies sell for European rentals typically do not cover stolen vehicles. Before you buy additional coverage for theft, check with your credit-card company and personal auto insurance—you may already be covered.

REQUIREMENTS

In the Netherlands, your own driver's license is acceptable. An International Driver's Permit is a good idea; it's available from the American or Canadian automobile association, and, in the United Kingdom, from the Automobile Association or Royal Automobile Club. These international permits are universally recognized, and having one in your wallet may save you a problem with the local authorities.

SURCHARGES

Before you pick up a car in Amsterdam and leave it in another city, **ask about drop-off charges or one-way service fees,** which can be substantial. Note, too, that some rental agencies charge extra if you return the car before the time specified in your contract. To avoid a hefty refueling fee, **fill the tank just before you turn in the car,** but be aware that gas stations near the rental outlet may overcharge.

CAR TRAVEL

A network of well-maintained superhighways and other roads covers the Netherlands, making car travel convenient. Major European highways leading into Amsterdam from the borders are E19 from western Belgium; E25 from eastern Belgium; and E22, E30, and E35 from Germany. Follow the signs for *Centrum* to reach center city. Traffic is heavy but not stationary at rush hour. A valid driver's license from your home country is all that is required to operate a vehicle.

AUTO CLUBS

➤ IN AUSTRALIA: **Australian Automobile Association** (☎ 06/247–7311).

➤ IN CANADA: **Canadian Automobile Association** (CAA, ☎ 613/247–0117).

➤ IN NEW ZEALAND: **New Zealand Automobile Association** (☎ 09/377–4660).

➤ IN THE U.K.: **Automobile Association** (AA, ☎ 0990/500–600), **Royal Automobile Club** (RAC, ☎ 0990/722–722 for membership, 0345/121–345 for insurance).

➤ IN THE U.S.: **American Automobile Association** (☎ 800/564–6222).

FROM THE U.K.

The **Channel Tunnel** provides the fastest route across the English Channel—35 minutes from Folkestone to Calais, or 60 minutes from motorway to motorway. Le Shuttle, a special car, bus, and truck train, departs frequently throughout the day and night. No reservations are necessary, although tickets may be purchased in advance from travel agents.

The Tunnel is reached from Exit 11a of the M20/A20. Drivers purchase tickets from toll booths, then pass through frontier control before loading onto the next available train. Unloading at Calais takes eight minutes. Five-day round-trip for a small car with passengers starts at £95 (low-season, night travel); high-season day travel is £135.

➤ CONTACTS: **Le Shuttle** (☎ 0990/353535 in the U.K.).

ROAD MAPS

Michelin maps are regularly updated and are the best Netherlands maps. They are available at newsdealers and bookshops. Free city maps are generally available at tourist offices, and more complete city guides can be bought in bookshops. Gas stations near borders generally sell a variety of more detailed maps.

RULES OF THE ROAD

Be sure to observe speed limits. In the Netherlands, the speed limit is 120 kph (74 mph) on superhighways, 100 kph (60 mph) on urban-area highways, and 50 kph (30 mph) on suburban roads. Driving is on the right.

For safe driving, go with the flow, stay in the slow lane unless you want to overtake, and make way for faster cars wanting to pass you. In cities and towns, approach crossings with care; local drivers may exercise the principle of priority for traffic from the right with some abandon.

CHILDREN & TRAVEL

CHILDREN IN AMSTERDAM

Be sure to plan ahead and **involve your youngsters** as you outline your trip. When packing, include things to keep them busy en route. On sightseeing days try to schedule activities of special interest to your children.

GROUP TRAVEL

When planning to take your kids on a tour, look for companies that specialize in family travel.

➤ FAMILY-FRIENDLY TOUR OPERATORS: **Families Welcome!** (✉ 92 N. Main St., Ashland, OR 97520, ☎ 541/482-6121 or 800/326-0724, FAX 541/482-0660).

Grandtravel (✉ 6900 Wisconsin Ave., Suite 706, Chevy Chase, MD 20815, ☎ 301/986-0790 or 800/247-7651) for people traveling with grandchildren ages 7-17.

HOTELS

Many hotels in Amsterdam allow children under a certain age to stay in their parents' room at no extra charge, but others charge them as extra adults; be sure to **ask about the cutoff age for children's discounts.**

➤ BEST CHOICES: **Best Western** hotels (☎ 800/528-1234) in Amsterdam allow children under 12 to stay free when sharing a room with two paying adults. A maximum of five persons is allowed per room. The **Intercontinental** hotels (☎ 800/327-0200) and the **Hilton** hotels (☎ 800/445-8667) in Amsterdam allow one child of any age to stay free in his or her parents' room. Many hotels have family rooms.

CONSULATES AND EMBASSIES

➤ CONTACTS: **U.S. Consulate** (✉ Museumplein 19, Amsterdam, ☎ 020/664-5661). **British Consulate** (✉ Koningslaan 44, Amsterdam, ☎ 020/676-4343). **Canadian Embassy** (✉ 7 Sophialaan, The Hague, ☎ 070/361-4111). **Australian Embassy** (✉ Carnegielaan 4, 5217 KH, Den Haag, ☎ 070/310-8200). **New Zealand Embassy** (✉ Carnegielaan 10, 5217 KH, Den Haag, ☎ 070/346-9324). **Eire/Republic of Ireland Embassy** (✉ Dr Cuyperstraat 9, 2514 BA, Den Haag, ☎ 070/363-0993).

CONSUMER PROTECTION

Whenever possible, **pay with a major credit card** so you can cancel payment or be reimbursed if there's a problem, provided that you can supply documentation. This is the best way to pay, whether you're buying travel arrangements before your trip or shopping at your destination.

If you're doing business with a particular company for the first time, **contact your local Better Business Bureau and the attorney general's offices** in your state and the company's home state, as well. Have any complaints been filed?

Finally, if you're buying a package or tour, always **consider travel insurance** that includes default coverage (☞ Insurance, *below*).

➤ LOCAL BBBS: **Council of Better Business Bureaus** (✉ 4200 Wilson Blvd., Suite 800, Arlington, VA 22203, ☎ 703/276-0100, FAX 703/525-8277).

CUSTOMS & DUTIES

When shopping, **keep receipts** for all of your purchases. Upon reentering the country, **be ready to show customs officials what you've bought.** If you feel a duty is incorrect, appeal the assessment. If you object to the way your clearance was handled, get the inspector's badge number. In either case, first ask to see a supervisor, then write to the appropriate authorities, beginning with the port director at your point of entry.

ON ARRIVAL

There are no limits on goods (such as perfume, cigarettes, or alcohol) brought into the Netherlands from another EU country, provided that they are bought duty-paid (i.e., not in a duty-free shop) and are for personal use. If you enter from a non-EU country, or have purchased goods duty-free, you may bring in 200 cigarettes or 50 cigars or 100 small cigars or 250 grams of tobacco; 1 liter of alcohol (more than 22%) or 2 liters (less than 22%) of other liquid refreshments, 50 grams of perfume and .25 liters of cologne, 500 grams of coffee, 100 grams of tea, and other goods with a total value of up to Fl 125.

There are no restrictions regarding the import or export of currency.

ON DEPARTURE

To export Dutch flower bulbs, a health certificate issued by the Nederlandse Planteziektenkundige Dienst (Dutch Phytopathological Service) is required; these are provided with packages you buy from specialized flower bulb companies.

IN AUSTRALIA

Australia residents who are 18 or older may bring back $A400 worth of souvenirs and gifts (including jewelry), 250 cigarettes or 250 grams of tobacco, and 1,125 ml of alcohol (including wine, beer, and spirits). Residents under 18 may bring back $A200 worth of goods.

➤ INFORMATION: **Australian Customs Service** (Regional Director, ✉ Box 8, Sydney, NSW 2001, ☎ 02/9213–2000, ℻ 02/9213–4000).

IN CANADA

Canadian residents who have been out of Canada for at least 7 days may bring in C$500 worth of goods duty-free. If you've been away less than 7 days but more than 48 hours, the duty-free allowance drops to C$200; if your trip lasts 24–48 hours, the allowance is C$50. You may not pool allowances with family members. Goods claimed under the C$500 exemption may follow you by mail; those claimed under the lesser exemptions must accompany you. Alcohol and tobacco products may be included in the 7-day and 48-hour exemptions but not in the 24-hour exemption. If you meet the age requirements of the province or territory through which you reenter Canada, you may bring in, duty-free, 1.14 liters (40 imperial ounces) of wine or liquor *or* 24 12-ounce cans or bottles of beer or ale. If you are 16 or older you may bring in, duty-free, 200 cigarettes and 50 cigars.

You may send an unlimited number of gifts worth up to C$60 each duty-free to Canada. Label the package UNSOLICITED GIFT—VALUE UNDER $60. Alcohol and tobacco are excluded.

➤ INFORMATION: **Revenue Canada** (✉ 2265 St. Laurent Blvd. S, Ottawa, Ontario K1G 4K3, ☎ 613/993–0534, 800/461–9999 in Canada).

IN NEW ZEALAND
Homeward-bound residents with goods to declare must present themselves for inspection. If you're 17 or older, you may bring back $700 worth of souvenirs and gifts. Your duty-free allowance also includes 4.5 liters of wine or beer; one 1,125-ml bottle of spirits; and either 200 cigarettes, 250 grams of tobacco, 50 cigars, or a combo of all three up to 250 grams.

➤ INFORMATION: **New Zealand Customs** (✉ Custom House, 50 Anzac Ave., Box 29, Auckland, ☎ 09/359–6655, ☎ 09/309–2978).

IN THE U.K.
If you are a U.K. resident and your journey was wholly within the European Union (EU), you won't have to pass through customs when you return to the United Kingdom. If you plan to bring back large quantities of alcohol or tobacco, check EU limits beforehand.

➤ INFORMATION: **HM Customs and Excise** (✉ Dorset House, Stamford St., London SE1 9NG, ☎ 0171/202–4227).

IN THE U.S.
U.S. residents may bring home $400 worth of foreign goods duty-free if they've been out of the country for at least 48 hours (and if they haven't used the $400 allowance or any part of it in the past 30 days).

U.S. residents 21 and older may bring back 1 liter of alcohol duty-free. In addition, regardless of your age, you are allowed 200 cigarettes and 100 non-Cuban cigars. Antiques, which the U.S. Customs Service defines as objects more than 100 years old, enter duty-free, as do original works of art done entirely by hand, including paintings, drawings, and sculptures.

You may also send packages home duty-free: up to $200 worth of goods for personal use, with a limit of one parcel per addressee per day (and no alcohol or tobacco products or perfume worth more than $5); label the package PERSONAL USE, and attach a list of its contents and their retail value. Do not label the package UNSO-

LICITED GIFT, or your duty-free exemption will drop to $100. Mailed items do not affect your duty-free allowance on your return.

➤ INFORMATION: **U.S. Customs Service** (Inquiries, ✉ Box 7407, Washington, DC 20044, ☎ 202/927–6724; complaints, Office of Regulations and Rulings, ✉ 1301 Constitution Ave. NW, Washington, DC 20229; registration of equipment, Resource Management, ✉ 1301 Constitution Ave. NW, Washington DC 20229, ☎ 202/927–0540).

DISABILITIES & ACCESSIBILITY

The Netherlands leads the world in providing facilities for people with disabilities. Train and bus stations are equipped with special telephones, elevators, and toilets. Visitors can obtain special passes to ensure free escort service on Dutch trains. For general assistance at railway stations, contact the NS/Nederlandse Spoorwegen before 2 PM at least one day in advance, or by 2 PM Friday for travel on Saturday, Sunday, Monday, or public holidays. Modern intercity train carriages have wheelchair-accessible compartments, and many have a free Red Cross wheelchair available. Train timetables are available in Braille, and some restaurants have menus in Braille. Some tourist sites also have special gardens for visitors with vision impairments. For information on accessibility in Amsterdam, and for general information relevant to travelers with disabilities, contact the national organization, De Gehandicaptenraad.

Each year the **Netherlands Board of Tourism** (☞ Visitor Information, *below*) publishes a booklet listing hotels, restaurants, hostels and campsites, museums, and tourist attractions, as well as gas/petrol stations with 24-hour services and boat firms, with adapted facilities. For travelers with visual impairments, all Dutch paper currency is embossed with different symbols for each denomination. For information on tours and exchanges for travelers with disabilities, contact Mobility International Nederland.

➤ LOCAL RESOURCES: **NS/Nederlandse Spoorwegen** (✉ Netherlands Railways, ☎ 030/230–5566 weekdays 8–4). **De Gehandicaptenraad** (✉ Postbus 19152, 3501 DD Utrecht, ☎ 030/230–6603 or 030/231–3454). **Mobility International Nederland** (✉ Postbus 41, 9244 ZN Beetsterswaag, ☎ 0512/382–5586).

LODGING

➤ CONTACTS: Accessible rooms in Amsterdam are available at the **Hilton hotels** (☎ 800/531–5900).

MAKING RESERVATIONS

When discussing accessibility with an operator or reservations agent, **ask hard questions.** Are there any stairs, inside *or* out? Are there grab bars next to the toilet *and* in the shower/tub? How wide is the doorway to the room? To the bathroom? For the most extensive facilities meeting the latest legal specifications, **opt for newer accommodations,** which are more likely to have been designed with access in mind. Older buildings or ships may have more limited facilities. Be sure to **discuss your needs before booking.**

DISCOUNTS & DEALS

Be a smart shopper and **compare all your options** before making any choice. A plane ticket bought with a promotional coupon may not be cheaper than the least expensive fare from a discount ticket agency. For high-price travel purchases, such as packages or tours, keep in mind that what you get is just as important as what you save. Just because something is cheap doesn't mean it's a bargain.

CLUBS & COUPONS

Many companies sell discounts in the form of travel clubs and coupon books, but these cost money. You must use participating advertisers to get a deal, and only after you recoup the initial membership cost or book price do you begin to save. If you plan to use the club or coupons frequently, you may save considerably. Before signing up, find out what discounts you get for free.

➤ DISCOUNT CLUBS: **Entertainment Travel Editions** (⊠ 2125 Butterfield Rd., Troy, MI 48084, ☎ 800/445–4137; $20–$51, depending on destination). **Great American Traveler** (⊠ Box 27965, Salt Lake City, UT 84127, ☎ 801/974–3033 or 800/548–2812; $49.95 per year). **Moment's Notice Discount Travel Club** (⊠ 7301 New Utrecht Ave., Brooklyn, NY 11204, ☎ 718/234–6295; $25 per year, single or family). **Privilege Card International** (⊠ 237 E. Front St., Youngstown, OH 44503, ☎ 330/746–5211 or 800/236–9732; $74.95 per year). **Sears's Mature Outlook** (⊠ Box 9390, Des Moines, IA 50306, ☎ 800/336–6330; $19.95 per year). **Travelers Advantage** (⊠ CUC Travel Service, 3033 S. Parker Rd., Suite 1000, Aurora, CO 80014, ☎ 800/548–1116 or 800/648–4037; $59.95 per year, single or family). **Worldwide Discount Travel Club** (⊠ 1674 Meridian Ave., Miami Beach, FL 33139, ☎ 305/534–2082; $50 per year family, $40 single).

CREDIT-CARD BENEFITS

When you use your credit card to make travel purchases you may receive free travel-accident insurance, collision-damage insurance, and medical or legal assistance, depending on the card and the bank that issued it. American Express, MasterCard, and Visa provide one or more of these services, so **look at a copy of your credit card's travel-benefits policy.** If you are a member of an auto club, always **ask hotel and car-rental reservations agents about auto-club discounts.** Some clubs offer additional discounts on tours, cruises, and admission to attractions.

DISCOUNT RESERVATIONS

To save money, **look into discount-reservations services** with toll-free numbers, which use their buying power to get a better price on hotels, airline tickets, even car rentals. When booking a room, always **call the hotel's local toll-free number** (if one is available) rather than the central reservations number—you'll often get a better price. Always ask about special packages or corporate rates.

When shopping for the best deal on hotels and car rentals, **look for guaranteed exchange rates.** With your rate locked in, you won't pay more, even if the price goes up in the local currency.

➤ AIRLINE TICKETS: **Fly 4 Less** (☎ 800/359–4537). **Martinair** (☎ 800/627–8462) offers reduced-fare flights to Amsterdam seasonally from Los Angeles, Miami, Newark, Oakland, Orlando, Tampa, Toronto, Vancouver, and Winnipeg.

➤ HOTEL ROOMS: **Hotels Plus** (☎ 800/235–0909). **International Marketing & Travel Concepts** (☎ 800/790–4682). **Steigenberger Reservation Service** (☎ 800/223–5652). **Travel Interlink** (☎ 800/888–5898).

PACKAGE DEALS

Packages and guided tours can save you money, but don't confuse the two. When you buy a package, your travel remains independent, just as though you had planned and booked the trip yourself. Fly/drive packages, which combine airfare and car rental, are often a good deal. If you **buy a rail/drive pass,** you'll save on train tickets and car rentals. All Eurail- and Europass holders get a discount on Eurostar fares through the Channel Tunnel.

ELECTRICITY

To use your U.S.-purchased electric-powered equipment, **bring a converter and adapter.** The electrical current in the Netherlands is 220 volts, 50 cycles alternating current (AC); wall outlets take Continental-type plugs, with two round prongs.

If your appliances are dual-voltage, you'll need only an adapter. Don't use 110-volt outlets, marked FOR SHAVERS ONLY, for high-wattage appliances such as blow-dryers. Most laptops operate equally well on 110 and 220 volts and thus require only an adapter.

EMERGENCIES

In the Netherlands, dial **112** for police, ambulance, and fire. To contact the police directly, call ☎ 622–2222.

➤ DOCTORS AND DENTISTS: **Central Medical Service** (☎ 020/592–

3434); 24-hour service for all medical assistance, including names and opening hours of pharmacists and dentists.

➤ HOSPITAL EMERGENCY ROOMS: **Academisch Medisch Centrum** (⊠ Meibergdreef 9, ☎ 020/566–9111). **Onze Lieve Vrouwe Gasthuis** (⊠ 1e Oosterparkstraat 279, ☎ 020/599–9111). **VU Ziekenhuis** (⊠ De Boelelaan 1117, ☎ 020/444–4444).

GAY & LESBIAN TRAVEL

The Netherlands is one of the most liberal countries in the world in its social and legal attitude toward gays and lesbians. The age of consent is 16, there are stringent anti-discrimination laws, and gay couples registered as living together have some of the same rights as heterosexual couples. At press time legislation was before parliament to fully legalize same-sex marriage. There are also many helpful gay and lesbian organizations in Amsterdam.

➤ RESOURCES: **COC Nederland** (⊠ Nieuwezijds Voorburgwal 68/70, 1012 SE Amsterdam, Netherlands, ☎ 020/623–4596). **Gay & Lesbian Switchboard** (☎ 020/623–6565). **SAD Schorerstichting** (⊠ P.C. Hooftstraat 5, 1071 BL Amsterdam, Netherlands, ☎ 020/662–4206).

➤ GAY- AND LESBIAN-FRIENDLY TRAVEL AGENCIES: **Corniche Travel** (⊠ 8721 Sunset Blvd., Suite 200, West Hollywood, CA 90069,

☎ 310/854–6000 or 800/429–8747, FAX 310/659–7441). **Islanders Kennedy Travel** (⊠ 183 W. 10th St., New York, NY 10014, ☎ 212/242–3222 or 800/988–1181, FAX 212/929–8530). **Now Voyager** (⊠ 4406 18th St., San Francisco, CA 94114, ☎ 415/626–1169 or 800/255–6951, FAX 415/626–8626). **Yellowbrick Road** (⊠ 1500 W. Balmoral Ave., Chicago, IL 60640, ☎ 773/561–1800 or 800/642–2488, FAX 773/561–4497). **Skylink Travel and Tour** (⊠ 3577 Moorland Ave., Santa Rosa, CA 95407, ☎ 707/585–8355 or 800/225–5759, FAX 707/584–5637), serving lesbian travelers.

HEALTH

MEDICAL PLANS

No one plans to fall ill while traveling, but it happens, so **consider signing up with a medical-assistance company.** Members receive doctor referrals, emergency evacuation or repatriation, 24-hour telephone hot lines for medical consultation, cash for emergencies, and other personal and legal assistance. Coverage varies by plan, so **review the benefits of each carefully.**

➤ MEDICAL-ASSISTANCE COMPANIES: **International SOS Assistance** (⊠ 8 Neshaminy Interplex, Suite 207, Trevose, PA 19053, ☎ 215/245–4707 or 800/523–6586, FAX 215/244–9617; ⊠ 12 Chemin Riantbosson, 1217 Meyrin 1, Geneva,

Switzerland, ☎ 4122/785–6464, FAX 4122/785–6424; ⊠ 10 Anson Rd., 14-07/08 International Plaza, Singapore, 079903, ☎ 65/226–3936, FAX 65/226–3937).

INSURANCE

Travel insurance is the best way to **protect yourself against financial loss.** The most useful plan is a comprehensive policy that includes coverage for trip cancellation and interruption, default, trip delay, and medical expenses (with a waiver for preexisting conditions).

Without insurance, you will lose all or most of your money if you cancel your trip, regardless of the reason. Default insurance covers you if your tour operator, airline, or cruise line goes out of business. Trip-delay covers unforeseen expenses that you may incur due to bad weather or mechanical delays. It's important to compare the fine print regarding trip-delay coverage when comparing policies.

For overseas travel, one of the most important components of travel insurance is its medical coverage. Supplemental health insurance will pick up the cost of your medical bills should you become sick or be injured while traveling. U.S. residents should note that Medicare generally does not cover health-care costs outside the United States, nor do many privately issued policies. Residents of the United Kingdom can buy an annual travel-insurance policy valid for most vacations taken during the year in which the coverage is purchased. If you are pregnant or have a preexisting condition, make sure you're covered. British citizens should buy extra medical coverage when traveling overseas, according to the Association of British Insurers. Australian travelers should buy travel insurance, including extra medical coverage, whenever they go abroad, according to the Insurance Council of Australia.

Always **buy travel insurance directly from the insurance company;** if you buy it from a cruise line, airline, or tour operator that goes out of business you probably will not be covered for the agency or operator's default, a major risk. Before you make any purchase, **review your existing health and home-owner's policies** to find out whether they cover expenses incurred while traveling.

➤ TRAVEL INSURERS: In the U.S., **Access America** (⊠ 6600 W. Broad St., Richmond, VA 23230, ☎ 804/285–3300 or 800/284–8300). **Travel Guard International** (⊠ 1145 Clark St., Stevens Point, WI 54481, ☎ 715/345–0505 or 800/826–1300). In Canada, **Mutual of Omaha** (⊠ Travel Division, 500 University Ave., Toronto, Ontario M5G 1V8, ☎ 416/598–4083, 800/268–8825 in Canada).

➤ INSURANCE INFORMATION: In the U.K., **Association of British Insur-**

ers (⊠ 51 Gresham St., London EC2V 7HQ, ☎ 0171/600–3333). In Australia, the **Insurance Council of Australia** (☎ 613/9614–1077, FAX 613/9614–7924).

LANGUAGE

In the Netherlands, Dutch is the official language, but almost everybody knows at least some English and many speak it very well. If you take a side trip to a rural area you may need a phrase book, at least until the residents overcome their shyness about using the English they know.

LODGING

Amsterdam offers a range of choices, from the major international hotel chains to family-run restored inns and historic houses.

Most hotels that cater to business travelers will grant substantial weekend and midsummer rebates. Always ask what's the best rate a hotel can offer before you book.

➤ RESERVATIONS: **Netherlands Reservation Center** (NRC, Postbus 404, 2260 AK, Leidschendam, ☎ 070/419–5500, FAX 070/419–5519, www.hotelres.nl) handles bookings for Amsterdam, as well as other cities in the Netherlands.

B&B RESERVATION AGENCIES

Should you arrive without a room, head for one of three VVV Logiesservice (VVV Accommodation Service) offices. This is a same-day hotel booking service that, for a modest charge of Fl 5, can help you find a room.

➤ ACCOMMODATION SERVICE: **VVV Logiesservice** (⊠ Platform 2 at Centraal Station; ⊠ Stationsplein 10; ⊠ Leidsestraat 106).

HOSTELS

No matter what your age, you can **save on lodging costs by staying at hostels.** Hostelling International (HI), the umbrella group for a number of national youth hostel associations, offers single-sex, dorm-style beds and, at many hostels, "couples" rooms and family accommodations. Membership in any HI national hostel association, open to travelers of all ages, allows you to stay in HI-affiliated hostels at member rates (one-year membership is about $25 for adults; hostels run about $10–$25 per night).

➤ HOSTEL ORGANIZATIONS: **Hostelling International—American Youth Hostels** (⊠ 733 15th St. NW, Suite 840, Washington, DC 20005, ☎ 202/783–6161, FAX 202/783–6171). **Hostelling International—Canada** (⊠ 400-205 Catherine St., Ottawa, Ontario K2P 1C3, ☎ 613/237–7884, FAX 613/237–7868). **Youth Hostel Association of England and Wales** (⊠ Trevelyan House, 8 St. Stephen's Hill, St. Albans, Hertfordshire AL1 2DY, ☎ 01727/855215 or 01727/845047, FAX 01727/844126); membership in the U.S. $25, in Canada C$26.75, in the U.K. £9.30).

MAIL

Airmail letters up to 20 grams (⅔ ounce) cost Fl 1.60 to the United States or Canada, Fl 1 to the United Kingdom; postcards to the United States or Canada cost Fl 1, to the United Kingdom 80¢. Aerograms cost Fl 1.30.

MONEY

CREDIT & DEBIT CARDS

The two types of plastic are virtually the same. Both will get you cash advances at ATMs worldwide if your card is properly programmed with your personal identification number (PIN). (For use in the Netherlands, your PIN must be four digits long.) Both offer excellent, wholesale exchange rates. And both protect you against unauthorized use if the card is lost or stolen. Your liability is limited to $50, as long as you report the card missing. When you want to rent a car, though, you may still need a credit card. Although you can always *pay* for your car with a debit card, some agencies will not allow you to *reserve* a car with one.

➤ ATM LOCATIONS: **Cirrus** (☎ 800/424–7787). **Plus** (☎ 800/843–7587) for locations in the United States and Canada, or visit your local bank.

➤ REPORTING LOST CARDS: To report lost or stolen credit cards, call

the following toll-free numbers: **American Express** (☎ 800/327–2177); **Diners Club** (☎ 800/234–6377); **Discover Card** (☎ 800/347–2683); **MasterCard** (☎ 800/307–7309); and **Visa** (☎ 800/847–2911).

CURRENCY

The official monetary unit of the Netherlands is the guilder, which may be abbreviated as Dfl, Fl, F, Hfl, and occasionally as NLG. There are 100 cents in a guilder, and coins are minted in denominations of 5, 10, and 25 cents, and 1, 2½, and 5 guilders. Bank notes are printed in amounts of 10, 25, 50, 100, 250, and 1,000 guilders. Bank notes in denominations of more than Fl 100 are seldom seen, and some shops refuse to accept Fl 1,000 notes. In winter 1999 the exchange rate was about 1.95 guilders to the dollar, 1.29 to the Canadian dollar, and 3.18 to the pound sterling. These rates fluctuate daily, so check them at the time of your departure.

EXCHANGING MONEY

For the most favorable rates, **change money through banks.** Although fees charged for ATM transactions may be higher abroad than at home, Cirrus and Plus exchange rates are excellent, because they are based on wholesale rates offered only by major banks. You won't do as well at exchange booths in airports or rail and bus stations, in hotels, in restaurants, or in stores, although you may find their hours more convenient. To avoid lines at airport exchange booths, **get a bit of local currency before you leave home.**

➤ EXCHANGE SERVICES: **Chase** *Currency To Go* (☎ 800/935–9935; 935–9935 in NY, NJ, and CT). **International Currency Express** (☎ 888/842–0880 on the East Coast, 888/278–6628 on the West Coast). **Thomas Cook Currency Services** (☎ 800/287–7362 for telephone orders and retail locations).

➤ IN AMSTERDAM: **GWK/ Grenswisselkantoren** (✉ Centraal Station, ☎ 020/627–2731).

TRAVELER'S CHECKS

Lost or stolen checks can usually be replaced within 24 hours. To ensure a speedy refund, buy your own traveler's checks—don't let someone else pay for them: irregularities like this can cause delays. The person who bought the checks should make the call to request a refund.

OPENING AND CLOSING TIMES

Banks are open weekdays from 8 or 9 to 4 or 5; post offices are open weekdays from 8:30 to 5 and often on Saturday from 8:30 to noon. Most national **museums** are closed on Monday, though the larger Amsterdam museums are open daily. **Pharmacies** are open weekdays from 8 or 9 to 5:30, with a rotating schedule in each city to cover nights and weekends.

Shops' hours, regulated by the government, are Monday from 1 to 6, Tuesday through Friday from 9 to 6, and Saturday from 9 to 5. Certain shops now have permission to open from noon to 5 on Sunday. Some branches of supermarkets now stay open until 7 or 8 on weekdays.

PACKING

LUGGAGE

How many carry-on bags you can bring with you is up to the airline. Most allow two, but the limit is often reduced to one on certain flights. Gate agents will take excess baggage—including bags they deem oversize—from you as you board and add it to checked luggage. To avoid this situation, make sure that everything you carry aboard will fit under your seat. Also, get to the gate early, and request a seat at the back of the plane; you'll probably board first, while the overhead bins are still empty. Since big, bulky baggage attracts the attention of gate agents and flight attendants on a busy flight, make sure your carry-on is really a carry-on. Finally, a carry-on that's long and narrow is more likely to remain unnoticed than one that's wide and squarish.

When flying internationally, note that baggage allowances may be determined not by piece but by weight—generally 88 pounds (40 kilograms) in first class, 66 pounds (30 kilograms) in business class, and 44 pounds (20 kilograms) in economy.

Airline liability for baggage is limited to $1,250 per person on flights within the United States. On international flights it amounts to $9.07 per pound or $20 per kilogram for checked baggage (roughly $640 per 70-pound bag) and $400 per passenger for unchecked baggage. You can buy additional coverage at check-in for about $10 per $1,000 of coverage, but it excludes a rather extensive list of items, shown on your airline ticket.

Before departure, **itemize your bags' contents** and their worth, and label the bags with your name, address, and phone number. (If you use your home address, cover it so that potential thieves can't see it readily.) Inside each bag, **pack a copy of your itinerary.** At check-in, **make sure that each bag is correctly tagged** with the destination airport's three-letter code. If your bags arrive damaged or fail to arrive at all, **file a written report with the airline before leaving the airport.**

PACKING LIST

The best advice for a trip to Amsterdam in any season is to pack light, be flexible, bring an umbrella (and trench coat with a liner in winter), and always have a sweater or jacket available. For daytime wear and casual evenings, turtlenecks and flannel shirts are ideal for winter, alone or under a sweater, and cotton shirts with sleeves are perfect in summer. Blue jeans are popular and are even sometimes worn to the office; sweat suits, however, are never seen outside fitness centers. For women, high heels are nothing but trouble on the cobblestone streets of Amsterdam, and sneakers or running shoes are a dead giveaway that you are an American tourist; a better choice is a pair of dark-color walking shoes or low-heeled pumps.

In your carry-on luggage **bring an extra pair of eyeglasses or contact lenses** and **enough of any medication you take** to last the entire trip. You may also want your doctor to write a spare prescription using the drug's generic name, since brand names may vary from country to country. **Never put prescription drugs or valuables in luggage to be checked.** To avoid customs delays, carry medications in their original packaging. And don't forget to copy down and carry addresses of offices that handle refunds of lost traveler's checks.

PASSPORTS & VISAS

When traveling internationally, **carry a passport even if you don't need one** (it's always the best form of I.D.), and make **two photocopies of the data page** (one for someone at home and another for you, carried separately from your passport). If you lose your passport, promptly call the nearest embassy or consulate and the local police.

ENTERING THE NETHERLANDS

All U.S., Canadian, U.K., Australian, Irish, and New Zealand citizens, even infants, need only a valid passport to enter the Netherlands for stays of up to 90 days.

PASSPORT OFFICES

The best time to apply for a passport or to renew is during the fall and winter. Before any trip, be sure to check your passport's expiration date and, if necessary, renew it as soon as possible.

➤ AUSTRALIAN CITIZENS: **Australian Passport Office**, Melbourne (☎ 131–232).

➤ CANADIAN CITIZENS: **Passport Office**, Ottawa (☎ 819/994–3500 or 800/567–6868).

➤ IRISH CITIZENS: **Passport Office**, Dublin (☎ 671–1633).

➤ NEW ZEALAND CITIZENS: **New Zealand Passport Office**, Wellington (☎ 04/494–0700 for information on how to apply, 0800/727–776 for information on applications already submitted).

➤ U.K. CITIZENS: **London Passport Office** (☎ 0990/21010), for fees and documentation requirements and to request an emergency passport.

➤ U.S. CITIZENS: **National Passport Information Center** (☎ 900/225–5674; calls are charged at 35¢ per minute for automated service, $1.05 per minute for operator service).

PUBLIC TRANSPORTATION

Amsterdam is a small city, and most major sites are within its central district. The canal-laced core is surrounded by concentric rings of 15th- to 17th-century canals, built following the pattern of earlier city walls and drainage ditches. Six roads link the city center with the more modern outer neighborhoods. Once you understand the fanlike pattern of Amsterdam's geography, you will have an easier time getting around. All trams and most buses begin and end their journeys at Centraal Station, sightseeing and shopping are focused at Dam Square, and the arts and nightlife are centered in the areas of Leidseplein, Rembrandtplein, and Waterlooplein.

BY TRAM, BUS, METRO

The transit map published by GVB (Gemeentelijk Vervoer Bedrijf/City transport company) is very useful. It's available at the GVB ticket office across from the central railway station, or at the VVV (☞ Visitor Information, *below*) offices next door. It is also reprinted as the center spread in *What's On in Amsterdam,* the fortnightly guide to activities and shopping published by the tourist office. The map shows the locations of all major museums, monuments, theaters, and markets, and it tells you which trams to take to reach them.

Single-ride tickets valid for one hour can be purchased from tram and bus drivers for Fl 3.25, but it is far more practical to buy a *strippenkaart* (strip ticket) that includes from 2 to 45 "strips," or ticket units. The best buy for most visitors is the 15-strip ticket for Fl 11.50. A new service for visitors is the Circle Tram 20, which rides both ways around a loop that passes close to most of the main sights and offers a hop-on, hop-off ticket for one–three days. By tradition, Dutch trams and buses work on the honor system: Upon boarding, punch your ticket at one of the machines situated in the rear or center section of the tram or bus. The city is divided into zones, which are indicated on the transit map, and it is important to punch the correct number of zones on your ticket (one for the basic tariff and one for each additional zone traveled). Occasional ticket inspections can be expected: A fine of Fl 60 is the price for "forgetting" to stamp your ticket.

➤ MAPS AND TICKET INFORMATION: **GVB** (main office; ⊠ Prins Hendrikkade 108–114, ☎ 020/551–4911).

SENIOR-CITIZEN TRAVEL

To qualify for age-related discounts, **mention your senior-citizen status up front** when booking

hotel reservations (not when checking out) and before you're seated in restaurants (not when paying the bill). Note that discounts may be limited to certain menus, days, or hours. When renting a car, **ask about promotional car-rental discounts,** which can be cheaper than senior-citizen rates.

The Radisson SAS hotel in Amsterdam offers a 25% reduction off the rack rate to senior citizens over 65. For other hotels, check on the availability of senior rates when you book.

➤ EDUCATIONAL PROGRAMS: **Elderhostel** (⊠ 75 Federal St., 3rd Floor, Boston, MA 02110, ☎ 617/426–8056). **Interhostel** (⊠ University of New Hampshire, 6 Garrison Ave., Durham, NH 03824, ☎ 603/862–1147 or 800/733–9753, FAX 603/862–1113).

➤ HOTEL INFORMATION: **Radisson SAS Hotels** (☎ 800/333–3333).

SIGHTSEEING TOURS

BY BIKE

From April through October, guided three-hour bike trips through the central area of Amsterdam are available through Yellow Bike. **Let's Go** tours (☞ Contact the VVV in Visitor Information, *below*) takes you out of the city-center by train before introducing you to the safer cycling of the surrounding countryside. Their tours include Edam and Volendam, Naarden and Muiden and, in season, a Tulip Tour.

➤ BIKE TOUR OPERATORS: **Yellow Bike** (✉ Nieuwezijds Kolk 29, ☎ 020/620–6940).

BY BOAT
Several boat trips to museums are available.

➤ BOAT TOUR OPERATORS: **Canalbus** (✉ Nieuwe Weteringschans 24, ☎ 020/623–9886), which makes six stops along two different routes between Centraal Station and the Rijksmuseum, costs Fl 27.75 including a ticket for the Rijksmuseum and reductions for other museums. **Museumboot Rederij Lovers** (✉ Stationsplein 8, ☎ 020/622–2181) makes seven stops near 20 different museums. The cost is Fl 22 for a day ticket that entitles you to a 50% discount on admission to the museums.

BY BUS
Afternoon bus tours of the city operate daily. Itineraries vary, and prices range from Fl 25 to Fl 35. **Key Tours** (☞ Travel Agencies, *below*) offers a three-hour city tour that includes a drive through the suburbs and **Lindbergh Excursions** (☞ Travel Agencies, *below*) offers a 3½-hour tour, focusing on the central city and including a canal-boat cruise. However, it must be said that this city of narrow alleys and canals is not best appreciated from the window of a coach. Also, a number of visitors feel unhappy that part of some tours involves a visit to a diamond factory, where they feel pressured

into listening to a sales pitch. The same bus companies operate scenic trips to attractions outside the city.

BY CANAL
The quickest, easiest way to get your bearings in Amsterdam is to take a **canal-boat cruise**. Trips last from 1 to 1½ hours and cover the harbor as well as the main canal district; there is a taped or live commentary available in four languages. There are also dinner and candlelight cruises. Excursion boats leave from piers in various locations in the city every 15 minutes from March to October, and every 30 minutes in winter. Most launches are moored in the inner harbor in front of Centraal Station. Fares are about Fl 12–Fl 15.

➤ CANAL CRUISE OPERATORS: **Holland International** (✉ Prins Hendrikkade, opposite Centraal Station, ☎ 020/622–7788). **Meyers Rondvaarten** (✉ Damrak, quays 4–5, ☎ 020/623–4208). **Rederij D'Amstel** (✉ Nicolaas Witsenkade, opposite the Heineken Brewery, ☎ 020/626–5636). **Rederij Lovers** (✉ Prins Hendrikkade 26, opposite Centraal Station, ☎ 020/622–2181). **Rederij P. Kooij** (✉ Rokin, near Spui, ☎ 020/623–3810). **Rederij Noord/Zuid** (✉ Stadhouderskade 25, opposite Parkhotel, ☎ 020/679–1370). **Rederij Plas** (✉ Damrak, quays 1–3, ☎ 020/624–5406).

BY FOOT

The VVV (☞ Visitor Information, *below*) maintains lists of personal guides and guided walking tours for groups in and around Amsterdam and can advise you on making arrangements. The costs are from Fl 208 for a half day and Fl 333 for a full day. The tourist office also sells brochures outlining easy-to-follow self-guided theme tours through the central part of the city. Among them are "A Journey of Discovery Through Maritime Amsterdam," "A Walk Through the Jordaan," "Jewish Amsterdam," and "Rembrandt and Amsterdam."

➤ ART AND ARCHITECTURE TOURS: **Artifex** (⊠ Herengracht 342, 1016 CG, ☎ 020/620–8112). **Stichting Arttra** (⊠ Staalstraat 28, 1011 JM, ☎ 020/625–9303). **Archivisie** (⊠ Postbus 14603, 1001 LC, ☎ 020/625–8908).

➤ AUDIO TOURS: **Audio Tours** (⊠ Oude Spiegelstraat 9, behind Dam Palace, ☎ 020/421–5580) allows you to wander at your own pace with their 2–3 hour cassette-tape tours (with a map just in case you lose track) for Fl 15 per tour, plus a Fl 100 returnable deposit. There are three different tours available.

➤ JEWISH QUARTER TOURS: For information, contact the **Joods Historisch Museum** (⊠ Jonas Daniel Meyerplein 2–4, Postbus 16737, 1001 RE, ☎ 020/626–9945, ℻ 020/624–1721).

STUDENT TRAVEL

TRAVEL AGENCIES

To save money, **look into deals available through student-oriented travel agencies.** To qualify you'll need a bona fide student I.D. card. Members of international student groups are also eligible.

➤ STUDENT I.D.S & SERVICES: **Council on International Educational Exchange** (⊠ CIEE, 205 E. 42nd St., 14th Floor, New York, NY 10017, ☎ 212/822–2600 or 888/268–6245, ℻ 212/822–2699), for mail orders only, in the United States. **Travel Cuts** (⊠ 187 College St., Toronto, Ontario M5T 1P7, ☎ 416/979–2406 or 800/667–2887) in Canada.

➤ STUDENT TOURS: **AESU Travel** (⊠ 2 Hamill Rd., Suite 248, Baltimore, MD 21210-1807, ☎ 410/323–4416 or 800/638–7640, ℻ 410/323–4498).

Contiki Holidays (⊠ 300 Plaza Alicante, Suite 900, Garden Grove, CA 92840, ☎ 714/740–0808 or 800/266–8454, ℻ 714/740–2034).

TAXES

HOTELS

All hotels in the Netherlands charge a 6% Value Added Tax, which is usually included in the quoted room price. In addition, some local city authorities impose a "tourist tax." This is added to your bill, but usually amounts to just an extra dollar or two a day.

VALUE-ADDED TAX (V.A.T.)

In the Netherlands a sales tax (BTW/VAT) of 17.5% is added to most purchases, such as clothing, souvenirs, and car fuel. Certain items (books among them) fall into a 6% band, as do hotel tariffs and restaurant meals.

To get a VAT refund you need to be a resident outside the European Union and to have spent Fl 300 or more in the same shop on the same day. Provided that you personally carry the goods out of the country within 30 days, you may claim a refund. Systems for doing this vary. Some shops will credit your credit card account, but most require you to present some form of proof of purchase at the customs desk at Schiphol Airport on your way home. Most leading stores will issue you a "VAT cheque" as proof of purchase (and charge a commission for the service). Have these tax-refund forms stamped at customs as you leave the final European Union country on your itinerary; send the stamped form back to the store. Alternatively and for a simpler procedure, if you shop at a store that displays a Europe Tax Free Shopping sticker, ask for a refund check at the store, have it validated at customs at the airport, and claim a cash refund (minus 20% handling) at an ETS booth. The amount of the refund varies (some organizations deduct a commission), but a refund of 10%–15% is standard.

TAXIS

Taxi stands are at the major squares and in front of the large hotels. You can also call Taxicentrale, the central taxi dispatching office. Fares are Fl 5.60, plus Fl 2.80 per kilometer. A 5-km (3-mi) ride will cost about Fl 20.

➤ TAXIS: **Taxicentrale** (☎ 020/677–7777).

WATER TAXIS

A Water Taxi provides a novel, if pricey, means of getting about. Water taxis can be hailed anytime you see one cruising the canals of the city, or called by telephone. The boats are miniature versions of the large sightseeing canal boats, and each carries up to eight passengers. The cost is Fl 90 for a half hour, including pick-up charge, with a charge of Fl 30 per 15-minute period thereafter. The rate is per ride, regardless of the number of passengers.

➤ WATER TAXIS: **Water Taxi** (☎ 020/622–2181).

TELEPHONES

COUNTRY CODES

The country code for the Netherlands is 31. Numbers with 0800 or 0900 codes are generally information numbers; the former free, the latter a charged service. When dialing a Dutch number from abroad, drop the initial 0 from the local area code.

The area code for Amsterdam is 020 (or 20 if you are calling from outside the Netherlands), and it is used only when you call from other parts of the Netherlands to Amsterdam. Within the immediate environs of any municipality you do not need to use an area code.

INTERNATIONAL CALLS

To call outside the Netherlands, dial 00 followed by the country code (1 for the United States and Canada, 44 for the United Kingdom), area code, and number.

AT&T, MCI, and Sprint international access codes make calling the United States relatively convenient, but you may find the local access number blocked in many hotel rooms. First ask the hotel operator to connect you. If the hotel operator balks, ask for an international operator, or dial the international operator yourself. One way to improve your odds of being connected to your long-distance carrier is to travel with more than one company's calling card (a hotel may block Sprint, for example, but not MCI). If all else fails, call from a pay phone in the hotel lobby.

➤ ACCESS CODES: **AT&T Direct** (☎ 0800/022–9111). **MCI World-Phone** (☎ 0800/022–9122). **Sprint International Access** (☎ 0800/022–9119).

LOCAL CALLS

Coin-operated telephones are becoming a rarity in the Netherlands, except in bars and cafés; most public phones take KPN (Dutch telephone company) phone cards, available from Fl 10, and credit cards.

OPERATORS AND INFORMATION

Dial 0900/8008 for **directory inquiries** within the Netherlands, 0900/8418 for numbers elsewhere. Both services cost about Fl 1 per minute. Operators speak English.

TIPPING

Service is included in the prices you pay, though it is customary to round up to the nearest guilder or two on small bills, and up to the nearest 5, 10, or even 25 guilders for good service on large bills.

TOUR OPERATORS

Buying a prepackaged tour or independent vacation can make your trip less expensive and more hassle-free. Because everything is prearranged, you'll spend less time planning.

Operators that handle several hundred thousand travelers per year can use their purchasing power to give you a good price. Their high volume may also indicate financial stability. But some small companies provide more personalized service; because they tend to specialize, they may also be more knowledgeable about a given area.

BOOKING WITH AN AGENT

Travel agents are excellent resources. In fact, large operators accept bookings made only through travel agents. But it's a good idea to **collect brochures from several agencies,** because some agents' suggestions may be influenced by relationships with tour and package firms that reward them for volume sales. If you have a special interest, **find an agent with expertise in that area**; ASTA (☞ Travel Agencies, *below*) has a database of specialists worldwide.

Make sure your travel agent knows the accommodations and other services. Ask about the hotel's location, room size, beds, and whether it has a pool, room service, or programs for children, if you care about these. Has your agent been there in person or sent others you can contact? **Do some homework on your own,** too: Local tourism boards can provide information about lesser-known and small-niche operators, some of which may sell only direct.

BUYER BEWARE

Each year consumers are stranded or lose their money when tour operators—even very large ones with excellent reputations—go out of business. So **check out the operator.** Find out how long the company has been in business, and ask several travel agents about its reputation. If the package or tour you are considering is priced lower than in your wildest dreams, **be skeptical.** Try to **book with a company that has a consumer-protection program.** If the operator has such a program, you'll find infor-

mation about it in the company's brochure. If the operator you are considering does not offer some kind of consumer protection, then ask for references from satisfied customers.

In the United States, members of the National Tour Association and United States Tour Operators Association are required to set aside funds to cover your payments and travel arrangements in case the company defaults. It's also a good idea to choose a company that participates in the American Society of Travel Agents' Tour Operator Program (TOP). This gives you a forum if there are any disputes between you and your tour operator; ASTA will act as mediator.

➤ TOUR-OPERATOR RECOMMENDATIONS: **American Society of Travel Agents** (☞ Travel Agencies, *below*). **National Tour Association** (⊠ NTA, 546 E. Main St., Lexington, KY 40508, ☎ 606/226–4444 or 800/755–8687). **United States Tour Operators Association** (⊠ USTOA, 342 Madison Ave., Suite 1522, New York, NY 10173, ☎ 212/599–6599 or 800/468–7862, FAX 212/599–6744).

PACKAGES

Independent vacation packages are available from major tour operators and airlines. Jet Vacations offers packages that include a choice of hotels, car rentals, and sightseeing in Amsterdam. Northwest WorldVacations provides visitors to Amsterdam with hotel, car rental, and tour options for a minimum of two nights.

▶ TOUR PACKAGE OPERATORS: **Jet Vacations** (✉ 880 Apollo St., Suite 241, El Segundo, CA 90245). **Northwest WorldVacations** (✉ 5130 County Rd. 101, Minnetonka, MN 55345, ☎ 800/727–3005).

TRAIN TRAVEL

The city has several substations, but all major Dutch national, as well as European international, trains arrive at and depart from Centraal Station. The station also houses the travel information office of NS/Nederlandse Spoorwagen (Netherlands Railways) and their international rail office.

The modern, clean trains have first- and second-class coaches and no-smoking and smoking cars. Rail fares are based upon distance; there are one-way fares, day-return fares for same-day round-trip travel, and multiday fares; bicycles may be carried aboard for a nominal fee. Children under 3 travel free and children under 11 are charged Fl 1 if they are accompanied by an adult.

▶ SCHEDULE INFORMATION: **Centraal Station** (☎ 0900/9292, 75¢ per minute, for local and national service information; 0900/9296, 50¢ per minute, for international). **NS/Nederlandse Spoorwagen** (Netherlands Railways; ☎ 0900/9292, costs 75¢ per minute).

FROM THE U.K.

British Rail International runs three trains a day from London to Amsterdam. Eurostar high-speed train service whisks riders through the **Chunnel** (☞ Car Travel, *above*) between stations in Paris (Gare du Nord) and London (Waterloo) in three hours, and between London and Brussels (Midi) in 3¼ hours. There are eight connecting services a day, including the high-speed Thalys, from Amsterdam Centraal Station to the Eurostar. Tickets for these services are available from international ticket counters at Dutch railway stations. Eurostar and Thalys tickets are available in the United Kingdom through British Rail International and in North America through Rail Europe and BritRail Travel.

▶ SCHEDULE AND TICKET INFORMATION: **British Rail International** (London/Victoria Station, ☎ 0171/834–2345 or 0171/828–0892 for credit-card bookings). **BritRail Travel** (☎ 800/677–8585 in the U.S., 800/555–2748 in Canada). **Eurostar** (☎ 0345/881881 in the U.K., 800/942–4866 in the U.S., 800/361–7245 in Canada). **Rail Europe** (☎ 800/942–4866). **Thalys** (✉ ☎ 0900/9228 in the Netherlands).

TRAVEL AGENCIES

A good travel agent puts your needs first. Look for an agency that has been in business at least five years, emphasizes customer service, and has someone on staff who specializes in your destination. In addition, **make sure the agency belongs to a professional trade organization,** such as ASTA in the United States. If your travel agency is also acting as your tour operator, *see* Buyer Beware in Tour Operators, *above.*

➤ AGENT REFERRALS: **American Society of Travel Agents** (ASTA, ☎ 800/965–2782 24-hr hot line, ℻ 703/684–8319). **Association of British Travel Agents** (✉ 55–57 Newman St., London W1P 4AH, ☎ 0171/637–2444, ℻ 0171/637–0713). **Association of Canadian Travel Agents** (✉ 1729 Bank St., Suite 201, Ottawa, Ontario K1V 7Z5, ☎ 613/521–0474, ℻ 613/521–0805). **Australian Federation of Travel Agents** (☎ 02/9264–3299). **Travel Agents' Association of New Zealand** (☎ 04/499–0104).

➤ AMSTERDAM AGENCIES: **American Express International** (✉ Damrak 66, ☎ 020/520–7777). **Thomas Cook** (✉ Damrak 1, ☎ 020/620–3236). **Holland International Travel Group** (✉ Dam 6, ☎ 020/622–2550). **Key Tours** (✉ Dam 19, ☎ 020/623–5051). **Lindbergh Excursions** (✉ Damrak 26, ☎ 020/622–2766). For student travel, **NBBS** (✉ Rokin 38, ☎ 020/624–0989).

VISITOR INFORMATION

TOURIST INFORMATION
The **Netherlands Board of Tourism** office maintains a data bank for special-interest travel, including specialized tours for senior citizens, gay and lesbian travelers, and travelers with disabilities.

➤ IN AMSTERDAM: The **VVV** (Amsterdam Tourist Office; ✉ Spoor 2/Platform 2, Centraal Station; ✉ Stationsplein 10, opposite Centraal Station; ✉ Leidsestraat 106, near Leideseplein; ✉ Stadionplein; ✉ Schiphol Airport; ☎ 0900/400–4040, Fl 1 per minute, weekdays 9–5, ℻ 020/625–2869).

➤ IN THE NETHERLANDS: The **Netherlands Board of Tourism** (✉ Postbus 458, 2260 MG, Leidschendam, The Netherlands).

➤ IN THE U.S.: The **Netherlands Board of Tourism** (✉ 355 Lexington Ave., 21st floor, New York, NY 10017, ☎ 212/370–7360 or 888/464–6552, ℻ 212/370–9507, www.goholland.com; ✉ 225 N. Michigan Ave., Suite 1854, Chicago, IL 60601, ☎ 312/819–1500, ℻ 312/819–1740; ✉ 9841 Airport Blvd., Suite 710, Los Angeles, CA 90045, ☎ 310/348–9339, ℻ 310/348–9344; for brochures, ☎ 888/464–6552).

➤ IN CANADA: The **Netherlands Board of Tourism** (✉ 25 Adelaide St. E, Suite 710, Toronto, Ontario M5C 1Y2, ☎ 416/363–1577, ℻ 416/363–1470).

➤ IN THE U.K.: The **Netherlands Board of Tourism** (✉ 25–28 Buckingham Gate, London SW1E 6LB, ☎ 0171/828–7900 or 0891/717–777 from UK).

WHEN TO GO

The best times to visit Amsterdam are late spring—when the northern European days are long and the summer crowds have not yet filled the beaches, the highways, or the museums—and in fall.

Amsterdam's high season begins in late March to late April, when the tulips come up, and runs through October, when the Dutch celebrate their Autumn Holiday. June, July, and August are the most popular months with both international visitors and the Dutch themselves. The cultural season lasts from September to June, but there are special cultural festivals and events scheduled in summer months.

Amsterdam has a mild maritime climate, with bright, clear summers and damp, overcast winters. The driest months are from February through May; the sunniest, May through August.

CLIMATE

What follows are average daily maximum and minimum temperatures for Amsterdam.

AMSTERDAM

Jan.	40F	4C	May	61F	16C	Sept.	65F	18C
	34	1		50	10		56	13
Feb.	41F	5C	June	65F	18C	Oct.	56	13C
	34	1		56	13		49	9
Mar.	47F	8C	July	70F	21C	Nov.	47F	8C
	38	3		59	15		41	5
Apr.	52F	11C	Aug.	68F	20C	Dec.	41F	5C
	43	6		59	15		36	2

1 Destination: Amsterdam

CULTURE, CHARM, AND CONTRADICTION

AMSTERDAM is a city with a split personality: It's a gracious, formal cultural center built on canals, and it's the most offbeat metropolis in the world. There is an incomparable romance about the canals at night, and a depth of cultural heritage in its great art museums; but there is also a houseboat crawling with stray cats permanently parked in front of an elegant gabled canal house, and prostitutes display their wares in the windows facing the city's oldest church. Only in Amsterdam can you marvel at the acoustics of the Concertgebouw one evening and be greeted by a hurdy-gurdy barrel organ pumping out happy tunes on the shopping street the next morning.

Amsterdam's museums are filled with some of the best art in the western world. There are the home-grown Old Masters and Van Gogh in the galleries and art museums, as well as works by artists such as Georg Breitner, who roamed Amsterdam with his friend Vincent van Gogh and produced atmospheric scenes of the city at night and in winter. There's also a wealth of contemporary art. Long an inspiration for genera-tions of artists, the attractive canals and gabled houses are a popular subject for today's Sunday painters.

You can skim the surface of the museums and get a glimpse of the canals in two to three days, but to really savor the city's charm, you need a week or more. The city is best in the spring when the parks and window boxes are filled with flowers and you can get a clear view of the gables between the branches of trees not yet in full leaf. Winters can be icy, with biting winds, but one of the compensations—if the canals freeze over—is ice skating. Amsterdam's best festival is Queen's Day, a street party on April 30 to celebrate the queen's birthday. June sees the star-studded Holland Festival of the Arts, which is part of a longer Amsterdam Arts Adventure, lasting well into the summer.

QUICK TOURS

If you're here for just a short stay, you need to plan carefully so you don't miss the must-see sights. The following itineraries outline major attractions throughout the city and will help you structure your visit efficiently. Each is intended to take about four hours—perfect to fill a free morning or afternoon. For more information about individual sights, *see* Chapter 2.

Centraal Station to the Waterlooplein

Leaving the Centraal Station, turn left on Oosterdokskade and head across the single-span pedestrian suspension bridge to the **newMetropolis Science and Technology Center.** The center's rooftop terrace offers a superb vista of the city, with a plan marking out the main sights. Next, bear right along the Prins Hendrikkade and cross the road to the broad, tree- and houseboat-lined **Oude Schans** canal. Passing the **Montelbaanstoren,** part of the city's early defenses, follow the canal to the sluice gates. To the left is the **Museum het Rembrandthuis,** where Rembrandt once lived and worked. After touring the museum, stroll through the stalls of the nearby **Waterlooplein flea market.** This district looks especially vivid in clear, bright morning light.

From the Dam to the Jordaan

In contrast to the din of the **Dam** (Dam Square), silence reigns within the thick-walled chambers of the **Het Koninklijk Paleis te Amsterdam** (Royal Palace, Amsterdam). From the majesty of this Golden Age remnant, head up the Raadhuisstraat to the Keizersgracht intersection; here the **Westerkerk tower** stands as a beacon, topped with the crown of Emperor Maximilian. For a thought-provoking history lesson, turn right up the Prinsengracht and visit the **Anne Frankhuis** (Anne Frank House). Afterward, weave your way through the Jordaan's myriad boutiques, brown cafés, and artisans' workshops, starting on the opposite side of the canal.

Museums Galore

From the Muntplein, at the intersection of the Singel and Amstel rivers, head south down the Vijzelstraat and turn right onto the Herengracht canal. After stopping to view the elegant mansions, take the first street on your left, the Nieuwe Spiegelstraat, from where you can see the neo-Gothic towers of the **Rijksmuseum.** You could spend a whole afternoon gazing at the museum's world-famous collection of Dutch art or continue through the central passageway to the Museumplein. Straight ahead is the **Concertgebouw** (concert building), with the **Van Gogh Museum** and the **Stedelijk Museum** to the right of the landscaped square; for the museum-lover, this art extravaganza is a holiday in itself.

Shops and Secrets

Starting from the Centraal Station, flow with the masses down the Damrak thoroughfare, past the redbrick mass of the **Beurs van Berlage** (Berlage Stock Exchange). Just before the Dam, stop at the grandiose **Bijenkorf department store.** Then cut diagonally across the square to the pedestrian-only **Kalverstraat,** where you'll find an abundance of inexpensive clothing. For an escape from the thronging shoppers and screeching trams, continue down the street to the elegant, 17th-century buildings of the **Amsterdam Historisch Museum.** Pass through the covered gallery to the idyllic **Begijnhof.** From the courtyard you can re-emerge into the modern world at **Spui** square and sit down for a well-deserved coffee on one of many café terraces.

2 Exploring Amsterdam

THE CITY IS LAID OUT in concentric rings of canals around the old center, crosscut by a network of access roads and alley-like connecting streets; you can easily see most of the city on foot, but there are also trams and water taxis. A walk from the center (Centraal Station) directly down to the southern edge takes you through the heart of town to the museum district. To the east of the center of town lie the Old Town and the former Jewish Quarter, and to the west you'll find the charming Jordaan. The grandest canals form a semicircle around the entire area.

Numbers in the text correspond to numbers in the margin and on the Exploring Amsterdam map.

City of the Arts: From the Dam to the Golden Bend

From inauspicious beginnings as a small fishing settlement built beside a dam in a muddy estuary in the 13th century, Amsterdam had developed, by the 17th century, into one of the richest and most powerful cities in the world. This Golden Age left behind it a tide-mark of magnificent buildings and some of the greatest paintings in western art. Amsterdam's wealth of art—from Golden Age painters through Van Gogh up to the present day—is concentrated on the area around the grassy Museumplein, which also serves as the transition point between the central canal area and the modern residential sections of the city. On the way from the site of the original dam to the museum quarter, you encounter some of the grand mansions built over the ages by Amsterdam's prosperous merchants.

A Good Walk

Begin where Amsterdam began, at the seething hub of the **Dam** ①. On the south side, where Kalverstraat and Rokin meet the square, is **Madame Tussaud Scenerama** ②, a branch of the famous wax museum. For a taste of ancient cultures, take a turn in the **Allard Pierson Museum** ③ farther down Rokin, on the left. From the Dam, follow the busy pedestrian shopping street, Kalverstraat, south to the entrance to the **Amsterdam Historisch Museum** ④ (or get there through the Enge Kapelsteeg alley if you have visited the Allard Pierson Museum). Here you can get an enjoyable, easily accessible lesson on the city's past. Passing through the painting gallery of the Historisch Museum brings you to the entrance of the **Begijnhof** ⑤, a blissfully peaceful courtyard, formerly housing the Beguine lay sisters. Behind the Begijnhof you come to an open square, the Spui, lined with popular sidewalk cafés, and to the Singel, the first of Amsterdam's concentric canals. Cut through the canals by way of the romantic Heisteeg alley and its continuation, the Wijde Heisteeg, turning left down the Herengracht to the corner of Leidsegracht. This is part of the prestigious **Gouden Bocht** ⑥, the grandest stretch of canal in town. Carry on down the Herengracht to the Vijzelstraat and turn right to the next canal, the Keizersgracht. Cross the Keizersgracht and turn left to find the **Museum van Loon** ⑦, an atmospheric canal house, still occupied by the family that has owned it for centuries but open to the public. Turn back down Keizersgracht until you reach Nieuwe Spiegelstraat; take another right and walk toward Museumplein. Rising up in front of you is the redbrick, neo-Gothic splendor of the **Rijksmuseum** ⑧, housing the world's greatest collection of Dutch art. When you leave the Rijksmuseum, walk through the covered gallery under the building. Directly ahead is Museumplein itself; to your right is Paulus Potterstraat (look for the diamond factory on the far corner), where you'll find the **Van Gogh Museum** ⑨, which contains a unique collection of that tortured artist's work. Continuing along Paulus Potterstraat, at the corner of Van Baerlestraat, you reach the **Stedelijk Museum** ⑩, where you can see modern art from Picasso to the present. Just around the corner, facing the back of the Rijksmuseum across Museumplein, is the magnificent 19th-century concert hall, the **Concertgebouw** ⑪. A short walk back up along Van Baerlestraat will bring you to the **Vondelpark** ⑫—acre after acre of parkland alive with people in summer.

TIMING

To see only the buildings, allow about an hour. Expand your allotment depending on your interest in the museums en route. At minimum, each deserves 60–90 minutes. At the Rijksmuseum allow at least that just to see the main Dutch paintings. You could easily pass most of the day there if you want to investigate the entire collection.

8

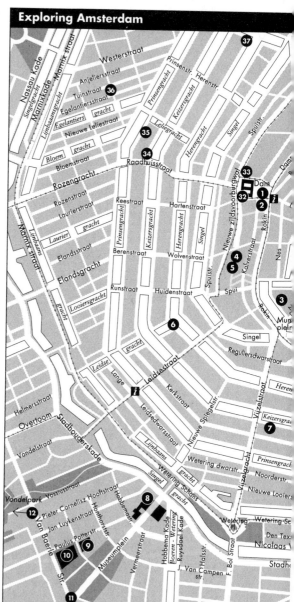

Exploring Amsterdam

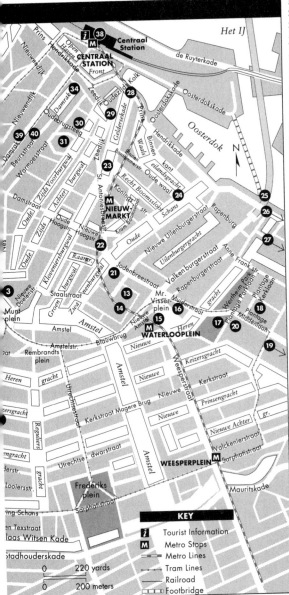

The best time to visit the Vondelpark is in the late afternoon or evening, especially in summer, as this is when the entertainment starts. In the busy season (July–September), lines at the Van Gogh Museum are long, so it's best to go early or allow for an extra 15 minutes' waiting time.

Sights to See

❸ Allard Pierson Museum. The fascinating archaeological collection of the University of Amsterdam is housed here, tracing the early development of Western civilization, from the Egyptians to the Romans, and of the Near Eastern cultures (Anatolia, Persia, Palestine) in a series of well-documented, interestingly presented displays. ⊠ *Oude Turfmarkt 127,* ☎ *020/525–2556.* ⌷ *Fl 7.50.* ☉ *Tues.–Fri. 10–5, weekends and holidays 1–5.*

★ **❹ Amsterdam Historisch Museum** (Amsterdam Historical Museum). Housed in a former orphanage, this museum traces the history of Amsterdam, from its beginnings in the 13th century as a marketplace for farmers and fishermen through the glorious period during the 17th century when Amsterdam was the richest, most powerful trading city in the world. A tall, skylighted gallery is filled with the guild paintings that document that period of power. In one of the building's tower rooms you can have a go on an old church carillon. ⊠ *Kalverstraat 92,* ☎ *020/523–1822.* ⌷ *Fl 11.* ☉ *Weekdays 10–5, weekends 11–5.*

★ **❺ Begijnhof** (Beguine Court). Here, serenity reigns just a block from the screeching of trams stopping next to the bustling **Spui** square. The Begijnhof is the courtyard of a residential hideaway, built in the 14th century as a conventlike residence for unmarried or widowed laywomen. It's typical of many found throughout the Netherlands. The court is on a square where you'll also find No. 34, the oldest house in Amsterdam and one of only two remaining wooden houses in the city center. After a series of disastrous fires, laws were passed in the 15th century forbidding the construction of buildings made entirely from timber. The small **Engelse Kerk** (English Church) in one corner of the square dates from 1400 and was used by the Pilgrim Fathers during their brief stay in Amsterdam in the early 17th century. ⊠ *Begijnhof 29,* ☎ *020/623–3565.* ⌷ *Free.* ☉ *Weekdays 11–4.*

NEED A
BREAK? The Spui is an open square that is the focal point of the University of Amsterdam. Several of the pubs and eateries here are good places to take a break, including **Caffe Esprit** (⊠ Spui 10, ☎ 020/622-1967), attached to the store of the same name. Try **Broodje van Kootje** (⊠ Spui 28, ☎ 020/623-7451) for a classic Amsterdam *broodje* (sandwich). The Spui is at the end of the alley that passes out of the Beguine Court.

⑪ Concertgebouw (Concert Building). The Netherlands' premier concert hall, the world-famous Concertgebouw, has been filled since the turn of the century with the music of the Royal Concertgebouw Orchestra, as well as visiting international artists. There are two concert halls in the building, Grote (large) and Kleine (small). The larger hall is one of the most acoustically perfect anywhere. You will recognize the building at once (it is topped with a lyre); enter through the glass extension along the side. There are no tours of the building, so you will need to buy a ticket to a concert to see beyond the broad lobby, or, if you visit on a Wednesday before 12:30 September–June, you can attend a free lunchtime concert. ⊠ *Concertgebouwplein 2–6,* ☎ *020/675–4411 (24-hr concert schedule and hot line) or 020/671–8345 (box office).*

NEED A
BREAK? **Small Talk** (⊠ Van Baerlestraat 52, ☎ 020/671-4864), because of its situation midway between the Concertgebouw and the Sweelinck Music Conservatory, is popular with music students, musicians, and visitors alike, who all pack in for coffee and apple pie or a light meal and a chat.

❶ Dam (Dam Square). The Dam, the official center of town, traces its roots to the 12th century, when wanderers from central Europe came floating in their canoes down the Amstel River and stopped to build a dam. Soon this muddy mound became the focal point of the small settlement of Amstelledamme and the location of the local weigh house. The Dam is still the official center of town. Once, ships could sail right up to the weigh house, along the Damrak. But in the 19th century the Damrak was filled in to form the street leading to Centraal Station, and King Louis Napoléon had the weigh house demolished in 1808 because it spoiled the view from his bedroom window in the palace across the way. The monument in the center of the square was erected in 1956 to commemorate the liberation of the Netherlands at the end of World War II. ⊠ *Follow Damrak south from Centraal Station; Raadhuisstraat leads from Dam to intersect main canals.*

❻ Gouden Bocht (Golden Bend). This stretch of the Herengracht, from the Leidsegracht to the Vijzelstraat, contains some of Amsterdam's most opulent 18th-century architecture. Construction of the main ring of canals, the Prinsengracht (Princes' Canal), the Keizersgracht (Emperors' Canal), and the Herengracht (Gentlemen's Canal), began during the Golden Age. In true Dutch egalitarian style, the most prestigious of the three was the Herengracht. The section of this canal stretching from Nieuwe Spiegelstraat to Leidsestraat is nicknamed the Golden Bend. Built by wealthy merchants, the houses are wide, with elaborate gables and cornices, richly decorated facades, and heavy, centrally placed doors—an imposing architecture that suits the bank headquarters of today as well as it did the grandees of yore. The most notable are numbers 475 (designed by Hans Jacob Husly in 1703); 485 (Jean Coulon, 1739); 493 and 527, both in the Louis XVI style (1770); and 284 (Van Brienen House, 1728), another ornate Louis XVI facade.

❷ Madame Tussaud Scenerama. A branch of the world-famous wax museum, this Madame Tussaud's—at Dam Square above the P&C department store—includes a life-size, 3-D rendering of a painting by Vermeer—a remarkable vision or a kitschy delight, depending on your sensibility. ⊠ *Dam 20,* ☎ *020/622–9949.* 🎟 *Fl 18.50.* ☉ *Sept.–June, daily 10–5:30; July–Aug., daily 9:30–7:30.*

★ ❼ Museum van Loon. The city's best look at life in the canal houses, the Museum van Loon is still a private residence for a descendant of one of Amsterdam's powerful families. Today, the house is filled with portraits, many of them traditional, paired marriage portraits and paintings of children. ⊠ *Keizersgracht 672,* ☎ *020/624–5255.* 🎟 *Fl 7.50.* ☉ *Fri.–Mon. 11–5.*

★ ❽ Rijksmuseum (State Museum). The Netherlands' greatest museum will celebrate the second centenary of its national art collection in 2000. It is home to Rembrandt's *The Night Watch* and many of the most beloved Vermeer, Hals, and Hobbema paintings extant. When architect P. J. H. Cuypers came up with the museum's extravagant design in the late 1880s, it shocked Calvinist Holland. Cuypers was persuaded to tone down some of the more ostentatious elements of his neo-Renaissance decoration and to curb the excesses of his soaring neo-Gothic lines—but, while the building was being constructed, he managed to visit the site and reinstate some of his ideas. The result is a magnificent, turreted building that glitters with gold leaf.

The Rijksmuseum has more than 150 rooms displaying paintings, sculpture, and objects from both the West and Asia, dating from the 9th through the 19th centuries. The primary collection is of 15th- to 17th-century paintings, mostly Dutch (the Rijksmuseum has the largest concentration of these masters in the world); there are also extensive holdings of drawings and prints from the 15th to the 20th centuries.

If your time is limited, then head directly for the Gallery of Honor on the upper floor, in which hangs Rembrandt's *The Night Watch,* as well as a selection of other well-known Rembrandt paintings, and works by Vermeer, Frans Hals, and other great Golden Age artists. A clockwise progression through the rooms of the adjoining East Wing takes you past works by some of the greatest Dutch painters of the 15th to the 17th centuries—meticulous still lifes, jolly tavern scenes, and rich portraits full of character.

The South Wing contains 18th- and 19th-century paintings, costumes and textiles, and the museum's impressive collection of Asian art, which includes some 500 statues of Buddha from all over the Orient.

The Rijksmuseum's collection of drawings and prints is far too vast to be displayed completely, and only a small selection is shown in the Print Room at any one time. Here you might catch a glimpse of Italian Renaissance sketches, Rembrandt engravings, or early-19th-century photographs.

Elsewhere in the museum you can wander through room after room of antique furniture, silverware, and exquisite porcelain, including Delftware. The 17th-century doll's houses—made as showpieces for wealthy merchant families—are especially worth seeing. ⊠ *Stadhouderskade 42,* ☎ *020/674–7000.* 🎫 *Fl 12.50.* ⊙ *Daily 10–5.*

❿ Stedelijk Museum (Municipal Museum). Hot and happening modern art has one of its most respected homes here at the Stedelijk. Works by such trendy contemporary artists as Jeff Koons are displayed alongside a collection of paintings and sculptures by the granddaddies of modernism: Chagall, Cézanne, Picasso, Monet, and others. Major movements that are well documented here are COBRA (Appel, Corneille), American pop art (Johns, Oldenburg, Liechtenstein), American action painting (Willem de Kooning, Pollock), and neo-realism (De Saint-Phalle, Tinguely). ⊠ *Paulus Potterstraat 13,* ☎ *020/573–2911.* 🎫 *Fl 9.* ⊙ *Daily 11–5.*

★ ❾ Van Gogh Museum. Based on a design by Gerrit Rietveld and opened in 1973, this museum venerates the short but prolific career of the 19th-century Dutch painter Vincent van Gogh. The collection of 200 paintings and 500 drawings by the artist ranges from the dramatic *Sunflowers* to ear-less self-portraits. The permanent collection also includes other important 19th-century artists. The year 1999 marks the 200th anniversary of Van Gogh's birth and the re-opening of the museum, closed for renovations in September 1998, with a new extension designed by Japanese architect Kisho Kurokawa. The new annex, to open in June along with the modernized Rietveld building, is a free-standing, multistory, oval structure, built in a bold combination of titanium and gray-brown stone and connected to the main galleries by an underground walkway. It provides space for temporary exhibitions, allowing more room to show the works of Van Gogh himself. ⊠ *Paulus Potterstraat 7,* ☎ *020/570–5200.* 🎫 *Fl 12.50.* ⊙ *Daily 10–5.*

⓬ Vondelpark. Known as the Green Lung of Amsterdam, the Vondelpark was first laid out in 1865 as a 25-acre "Walking and Riding Park." It soon expanded to cover some 120 acres. In the process, it was renamed after Joost van den Vondel, the "Dutch Shakespeare." Landscaped in the informal English style, the park is an irregular patchwork of copses, ponds, and fields linked by winding pathways. In good weather the park buzzes with activity. People come to roller skate and play tennis. Dutch families string up flags between the branches and party under the trees. Lovers stroll through the fragrant formal Rose Garden. Children sit transfixed by colorful acrobatics in the outdoor theater. Later, the clowns give way to jazz bands and cabaret artists who play well into the night, and the Vondelpark takes on the atmosphere of a giant outdoor café. From June to August free outdoor concerts and plays are performed at the open-air theater from Wednesday through Sunday.

Over the years a range of sculptural and architectural delights have made their appearance in the park. There's an elegant 19th-century bandstand, and the famous **Round Blue Teahouse,** a rare beauty of functionalist architecture, built beside the lake in 1937. **Picasso** himself donated a sculpture to commemorate the park's centenary in 1965. An elegant 19th-century entertainment pavilion has been converted into the **Nederlands Filmmuseum** (Netherlands Film Museum). Although there is no permanent exhibition, the museum has shows every day in its two cinemas, drawing on material from all over the world as well as from its substantial archive (which includes such gems as hand-tinted silent movies). On summer Saturdays, there are free outdoor screenings. ⊠ *Stadhouderskade. Filmmuseum, Vondelpark 3,* ☎ *020/589–1400.*

Historic Amsterdam: From the Jewish Quarter to Rembrandt's House

From the time in the 15th century when the diamond cutters of Antwerp first arrived to find refuge from the Spanish Inquisition, the area east of the Zwanenburgwal has traditionally been Amsterdam's Jewish Quarter. During the 16th and 17th centuries, Jewish refugees from Spain, Portugal, and Eastern Europe also found a haven in Amsterdam. By 1938, 10% of Amsterdam's population was Jewish, but this thriving community was decimated by the Nazi occupation.

The area to the north and northeast of the Jewish Quarter is the oldest part of Amsterdam. This is the site of Amsterdam's original harbor and the core of the Old Town, an area steeped in the history and romance of exotic trade and exploration, much of it conducted under the auspices of the wealthy Dutch East India Company (VOC).

A Good Walk

Start at what was once the heart of Amsterdam's Jewish Quarter, **Waterlooplein** ⑬. Today the square is dominated by the imposing modern **Muziektheater/Stadhuis** ⑭, which is surrounded by a large and lively flea market. East of Waterlooplein, on Jonas Daniël Meijerplein, is the **Joods Historisch Museum** ⑮, skillfully converted out of a number of old synagogues. Just to the east of that, on the corner of Mr. Visserplein and Jonas Daniël Meijerplein is the stately **Portugees Israelitische Synagoge** ⑯. Its interior is simple but awe-inspiring because of its vast size and floods of natural light. From here, you might like to make a short diversion, especially if you have children in tow. Tram 9 or 14 will take you along Plantage Middenlaan to the **Hortus Botanicus** ⑰, to the **Artis** ⑱ zoo (which was attractively laid out in parklike surroundings in the 19th century and has a well-stocked aquarium), and on to the **Tropenmuseum** ⑲, which has riveting displays on tropical cultures and a special children's section. On the way you might want to pop in to the **Verzetsmuseum** ⑳, which explains the Dutch resistance to the occupying forces, passive and active, during the Second World War. Alternatively, you can walk from the synagogue up Jodenbreestraat, where—in the second house from the corner by the Zwanenburgwal—you'll find the **Museum het Rembrandthuis** ㉑, the mansion where Rembrandt lived at the height of his prosperity, which now houses a large collection of his etchings. Cross the bridge to St. Antoniesbreestraat and follow it to the **Zuiderkerk** ㉒, whose rather Asian spire is the neighborhood's chief landmark. Take St. Antoniesbreestraat north to **Nieuwmarkt** ㉓. Take Koningsstraat to the Kromboomssloot and turn left, then right at Rechtboomssloot (both pretty, leafy canals) and follow it through this homey neighborhood, the oldest in Amsterdam, to Montelbaanstraat; turn left and cut through to the broad Oude Waal canal. Follow it right to the **Montelbaanstoren** ㉔, a tower that dates back to the 16th century. Up Kalkmarkt from the tower is Prins Hendrikkade, which runs along the eastern docks. Following Prins Hendrikkade east you enter the 20th century with a bang at the **newMetropolis Science**

& Technology Center ㉕. A little farther on is the **Nederlands Scheepvaartmuseum** ㉖ where there is a fascinating replica of an old Dutch East India ship. Across the bridge on Hoogte Kadijk is the **Museumwerf 't Kromhout** ㉗, where wooden sailing boats are still restored and repaired. If, on the other hand, you go west along Prins Hendrikkade to Gelderskade, you can see the **Schreierstoren** ㉘, where legend has it that women used to stand weeping and waiting for their men to return from sea. Follow Oudezijds Kolk, beside the Schreierstoren, south to the **Zeedijk** ㉙, in the 1980s the seedy haunt of drug dealers but now lined with restaurants, cafés, and galleries that form the heart of Chinatown. From Zeedijk, take Oudezijds Voorburgwal south to **Museum Amstelkring** ㉚, a tiny but atmospheric canal house that has a church hidden in its attic. Continue south on Oudezijds Voorburgwal through part of the red-light district to the **Oude Kerk** ㉛, Amsterdam's oldest church, which grew up haphazardly from the 14th to the 16th centuries. From here you can continue south on Oudezijds Voorburgwal through more of the red-light district to Damstraat and the Dam.

TIMING

To see only the buildings along the main route, block out an hour and a half. Detours to Artis and the Tropenmuseum will need an extra 30 minutes' traveling time; and to the Scheepvaartsmuseum and Museumwerf 't Kromhout, another 45 minutes. Museums along this route need at least a 30-minute visit, though the Museum Amstelkring and the Tropenmuseum deserve a little longer.

Note that the flea market does not operate on Sunday and that the children's section of the Tropenmuseum has very specific visiting times. Although the Zeedijk has been considerably cleaned up of late, it is still advisable to take care when visiting this area and the red-light district. Don't carry too many valuables, and avoid the district late at night.

Sights to See

⓲ **Artis** (The Amsterdam Zoo). Keep young travelers entertained with a visit to Amsterdam's zoo (known officially as the Natura Artis Magistra). Built in the mid-19th century, Artis is a 37-acre park that is home to a natural history museum, a zoo with an aviary, an aquarium, and a planetarium. A special Artis Express canal boat from the central railway station makes getting here fun. ✉ *Plantage Kerklaan 40,* ☎ *020/523–3400.* 🎟 *Fl 22.* ⊙ *Zoo, daily 9–5; planetarium, Mon. 12:30–5, Tues.–Sun. 9–5.*

⑰ Hortus Botanicus. The attractive botanical garden was laid out as an herb garden for doctors and pharmacists in 1638. It has since been expanded to incorporate a covered swamp and an ornamental garden, where 6,000 species are represented. ✉ *Plantage Middenlaan 2,* ☎ *020/625–8411.* 🎟 *Fl 7.50.* ⊙ *Apr.–Sept., weekdays 9–5, weekends and holidays 11–5; Oct.–Mar., weekdays 9–4, weekends and holidays 11–4.*

⑮ Joods Historisch Museum (Jewish Historical Museum). Four synagogues, dating from the 17th and 18th centuries, have been skillfully combined into one museum for documents, paintings, and objects related to the history of the Jewish people in Amsterdam and the Netherlands. Across from the entrance to the museum is a statue erected after World War II to honor a solidarity strike by Amsterdam's dock workers in protest of the deportation of Amsterdam's Jews during the war. ✉ *Jonas Daniël Meijerplein 2–4,* ☎ *020/626–9945.* 🎟 *Fl 8.* ⊙ *Daily 11–5.*

㉔ Montelbaanstoren (Montelbaans Tower). A slightly listing tower dating from 1512, when, perpendicular, it formed part of the city's defenses, the Montelbaanstoren now houses the City Water Office. Since 1878, this department has maintained the water levels in the canals and engineered the nightly flushing of the entire city waterway system, closing and opening the sluices to change the direction of the flow and cleanse the waters. (The canals remain murky green despite the process, due to algae.) The elegant clock tower was added early in the 17th century. ✉ *Oude Schans 2.*

㉚ Museum Amstelkring ("Our Lord in the Attic" Museum). This appears to be just another canal house, and on the lower floors it is, but the attic of this building contains something unique—a small chapel that dates from the Reformation in Amsterdam, when open worship by Catholics was outlawed. ✉ *Oudezijds Voorburgwal 40,* ☎ *020/624–6604.* 🎟 *Fl 10.* ⊙ *Mon.–Sat. 10–5, Sun. 1–5.*

★ **㉑ Museum het Rembrandthuis** (Rembrandt's House). One of Amsterdam's most remarkable sights, this was the house that Rembrandt, flush with success, bought for his family. He chose a house on what was once the main street of the Jewish Quarter because he felt that he could then experience daily and at firsthand the faces he would use in his religious paintings. Later Rembrandt lost the house to bankruptcy when he fell from popularity following his wife's death. He came under attack by the Amsterdam burghers, who refused to accept his liaison with his housekeeper. The house today is a museum of Rembrandt prints and etchings and includes one of his presses. ⊠ *Jodenbreestraat 4–6*, ☎ *020/624–9486*. 🖾 *Fl 7.50*. ☉ *Mon.–Sat. 10–5, Sun. and holidays 1–5*.

☪ **㉗ Museumwerf 't Kromhout** (Museum Wharf The Kromhout). One of Amsterdam's oldest shipyards is still redolent of tar, wood shavings, and varnish. Although the shipyard is run as a museum, old boats are still restored here. There's a whiff of diesel in the air, too. During the first part of the 20th century, 't Kromhout produced the diesel engine used by most Dutch canal boats. Models of old engines are on display. ⊠ *Hoogte Kadijk 147*, ☎ *020/627–6777*. 🖾 *Fl 3.50*. ☉ *Weekdays 10–4*.

⑭ Muziektheater/Stadhuis (Music Theater/Town Hall). A brick and marble complex known locally as the Stopera (from Stadhuis and opera), this is the cornerstone of the revival of the Jewish Quarter, which was derelict and devastated after World War II. Built as a home for everything from opera performances to welfare applications, it is a multifunctional complex that includes theaters, offices, shops, and even the city's wedding chamber (Dutch marriages all must be performed in the Town Hall, with church weddings optional). Feel free to wander through the lobbies; there is interesting sculpture as well as a display that dramatically illustrates Amsterdam's position below sea level. Tours of the backstage areas are run twice weekly. ⊠ *Waterlooplein 22*, ☎ *020/551–8054*. 🖾 *Fl 8.50 for tours*. ☉ *Open daily. Tours Wed. and Sat. at 3*.

☪ **㉖ Nederlands Scheepvaartmuseum** (The Netherlands Maritime Museum). Once the warehouse from which trading vessels were outfitted for their journeys, with everything from cannons to hardtack, the building now incorporates room after room of displays related to the development and power of the Dutch East and West Indies companies, as well as the Dutch fishing industry. Moored alongside the building at the east end of Amsterdam Harbor is a replica of the VOC (Dutch East India Company) ship *Amsterdam*. ⊠ *Kattenburgerplein 1, ☎ 020/523–2222. ✆ Fl 12.50. ☉ Tues.– Sat. 10–5, Sun. and holidays noon–5, June–Sept. also Mon. 10–5.*

⟳ ㉕ **newMetropolis Science & Technology Center.** Opened in early 1997, this is already a landmark, designed by Renzo Piano, the architect of the Pompidou Centre in Paris. The building's colossal, copper-clad volume rises from the harbor waters like the hull of a ship poking up into the skyline above the entrance to the IJ Tunnel in the city's Eastern Docks. Inside is a high-tech, hands-on world of historic, present-day, and futuristic technology. The rooftop café terrace offers a superb panoramic view across the city. ⊠ *Oosterdok 2, ☎ 0900/919–1100, 55¢ per minute. ✆ Fl 23.50. ☉ Sun.– Fri. 10–6, Sat. 10–9.*

㉓ **Nieuwmarkt** (New Market). Dating from the 17th century— when farmers from the province of Noord-Holland began setting up stalls here—the Nieuwmarkt soon became a busy daily market. The **Waag** (Weigh House) in the center of the square was built in 1488 and functioned as a city gate until the early 17th century, when it became the weighing house. One of its towers housed a teaching hospital for the academy of surgeons of the Surgeons' Guild. It was here that Rembrandt came to watch Professor Tulp in action prior to painting *The Anatomy Lesson*. Now the building is occupied by a restaurant. ⊠ *Bounded by Kloveniersburgwal, Geldersekade, and Zeedijk.*

㉛ **Oude Kerk** (Old Church). Amsterdam's oldest church, the Oude Kerk was built between 1366 and 1566 and restored from 1955 to 1979. It is a pleasing hodgepodge of styles and haphazard side buildings. Rembrandt's wife, Saskia, is buried here. Seminude women display their wares in the windows around the church square and along the surrounding canals—the neighborhood has doubled as a red-light district for nearly six centuries. ⊠ *Oudekerksplein 23, ☎ 020/625–8284. ✆ Fl 5. ☉ Apr.–Oct., Mon.–Sat. 11– 5, Sun. 1–5; Nov.–Mar., Fri.–Sun. 1–5.*

⑯ Portugees Israelitische Synagoge (Portuguese Israelite Synagogue). This noted synagogue was built between 1671 and 1675 by the Sephardic Jewish community that had emigrated from Portugal during the preceding two centuries. Its spare, elegantly proportioned wood interior has remained virtually unchanged since it was built and still is lighted by candles in two immense candelabra during services. ✉ *Mr. Visserplein 3,* ☎ *020/624–5351.* 💳 *Fl 5.* ☉ *Apr.–Oct., Sun.–Fri. 10–12:30 and 1–4; Nov.–Mar., Mon.–Thurs. 10–12:30 and 1–4, Fri. 10–12:30 and 1–3, Sun. 10–noon.*

㉘ Schreierstoren. Although today this is a shop for nautical instruments, maps, and books, during the 16th century it was a lookout tower for the women whose men were fishing at sea. This gave rise to the mistaken belief that the name meant "weeper's" or "wailer's" tower. But the word "Schreier" actually comes from an old Dutch word describing the position of the tower astride two canals. A plaque on the side of the building tells you that it was from this location that Henry Hudson set sail on behalf of the Dutch East India Company to find a shorter route to the East Indies, discovering instead Hudson's Bay in Canada and, later, New York harbor and the Hudson River. The Schreierstoren overlooks the old **Oosterdok** (Eastern Dock) of Amsterdam Harbor. ✉ *Prins Hendrikkade 94–95.*

⑲ Tropenmuseum (Museum of the Tropics). This museum honors the Netherlands' link to Indonesia and the West Indies. It is a magnificent tiered, galleried, and skylighted museum decorated in gilt and marble. Displays and dioramas portray everyday life in the world's tropical environments. ☾ Upstairs in the **Kindermuseum** (Children's Museum) children can participate directly in the life of another culture through special programs involving art, dance, song, and sometimes even cookery. Adults may visit the children's section, but only under the supervision of a child age 6–12. ✉ *Linnaeusstraat 2,* ☎ *020/568–8295.* 💳 *Fl 10; Kindermuseum, Fl 2.50.* ☉ *Mon. and Wed.–Thurs., 10–5, Tues. 10–9:30, weekends and holidays noon–5; Kindermuseum activities Wed. at 2 and 3:30, weekends at 12:30, 2, and 3:30.*

⑳ Verzetsmuseum (Museum of the Dutch Resistance). Here are displays explaining the Dutch resistance to the occupying forces, passive and active, during World War II. Opening in a new location in May 1999, the museum is poignantly close to the former **Schouwburg** theater on Plantage Middenlaan, which is now a memorial to the Jews who were assembled here before being sent to the concentration camps. ⊠ *Plantage Kerklaan 61,* ☎ *020/620–2535.* ☞ *Fl 8.* ☉ *Tues.–Fri. 10–5, weekends noon–5.*

⑬ Waterlooplein. The wooden pushcarts that were used when the flea market here began (before World War II) are gone, but the Waterlooplein remains a bustling shopping arena, wrapped around two sides of the Stopera (Music Theater/Town Hall complex). A stroll past the stalls provides a colorful glimpse of Amsterdam entrepreneurship in action, day in and day out, in every sort of weather. ⊠ *Waterlooplein.* ☉ *Weekdays 9–5, Sat. 8:30–5:30.*

NEED A BREAK? **Espressobar "Puccini"** (⊠ Staalstraat 21, ☎ 020/620-8458. ☉ Tues.-Sat. 8:30-8, Sun. 10-6) is a stylish breakfast and lunch venue, just across the water from the Waterlooplein flea market and the Muziektheater. You can get a full Continental breakfast or freshly made sandwiches with interesting fillings, while the cakes, some created in the superb *chocolaterie* next door, are mouthwatering treats.

㉙ Zeedijk. Once known throughout the country as the black hole of Amsterdam for its concentration of drug traffickers and users, Zeedijk is now the busy heart of the city's Chinatown, and there is even a Buddhist temple. The restored old buildings now house shops, restaurants, and galleries. No. 1 Zeedijk, a café, is one of only two timbered houses left in the city. ⊠ *Oudezijds Kolk (near Centraal Station) to Nieuwmarkt.*

㉒ Zuiderkerk (South Church). Built between 1603 and 1611 by Hendrick de Keyser, one of the most prolific architects of the Golden Age, this church is said to have inspired the great British architect Christopher Wren. The Zuiderkerk was one of the earliest churches built in Amsterdam in the Renaissance style and was the first in the city to be built for the Dutch Reformed Church. The city planning office maintains a display here that offers a look at the future of

Amsterdam. ⊠ *Zandstraat.* 🖼 *Free.* ⊙ *Tower: June–Oct., Wed. 2–5, Thurs.–Fri. 11–2, Sat. 11–4.*

The Canals: City of 1,001 Bridges

One of Amsterdam's greatest pleasures is also one of its simplest—a stroll along the canals. The grand, crescent-shape waterways of the *grachtengordel* (belt of canals) are lined with splendid buildings and pretty, gabled houses. But you can also wander off the main thoroughfares, along the smaller canals that crisscross them, sampling the charms of such historic city neighborhoods as the Jordaan.

A Good Walk

Begin at the busy **Dam** ①, where the imposing **Het Koninklijk Paleis te Amsterdam** ㉜ fills the western side of the square. The richly decorated marble interiors are open to the public when the queen is not in residence. To the right of the palace looms the Gothic **Nieuwe Kerk** ㉝. Circle around behind the palace, follow the tram tracks into the wide and busy Raadhuisstraat, and continue along it to the Westermarkt. The **Westerkerk** ㉞, on the right, facing the next canal, is another Amsterdam landmark, and Rembrandt's burial place. Make a right past the church and follow the Prinsengracht canal to the **Anne Frankhuis** ㉟, where you can visit the attic hideaway where Anne Frank wrote her diary. Continue north along the Prinsengracht. The neighborhood to your left, across the canal, is the **Jordaan** ㊱, full of curious alleys and pretty canals, intriguing shops and cafés. At the intersection of the Prinsengracht and Brouwersgracht, turn right onto the **Brouwersgracht** ㊲, which many believe is the most beautiful canal in Amsterdam. Cross the canal and follow it back to the Singel. On the other side, follow the tram tracks to the left toward the harbor. Ahead of you is the palatial **Centraal Station** ㊳. From Centraal Station the **Damrak** ㊴ leads past the **Beurs van Berlage** ㊵— the building that is seen as Amsterdam's first significant venture into modern architecture—and back to the Dam.

TIMING

It is difficult to say how long this walk will take as it leads you through areas that invite wandering and the exploration of side streets. At a brisk and determined pace, you can manage the route in about an hour. But you could also easily while away an afternoon in the Jordaan, or take a leisurely stroll along the Prinsengracht. Allow a minimum of half an hour each for the Royal Palace and the Anne Frank House. Waiting in line to get into the Anne Frank House can add another 10–20 minutes (get there early to beat the midday crowds).

The best time for canal walks is in late afternoon and early evening—or early in the morning, when the mists still hang over the water. If you're planning to go shopping in the Jordaan, remember that shops in the Netherlands are closed Monday morning. With its many restaurants and cafés, the Jordaan is also fun to visit at night.

Sights to See

★ ㉟ **Anne Frankhuis** (Anne Frank House). This unimposing canal house where two Jewish families hid from the Nazis for more than two years during World War II is one of the most frequently visited places in the world. The families were eventually discovered and sent to concentration camps, but young Anne's diary survived as a detailed record of their life in hiding. If you have time to see nothing else in Amsterdam, don't miss a visit to this house. The swinging bookcase that hid the door to the secret attic apartment is still there, you can walk through the rooms where Anne and her family lived, and there is also an exhibition on racism and oppression. ⊠ *Prinsengracht 263,* ☎ *020/556–7100.* ⚏ *Fl 10.* ☉ *June–Aug., Mon.–Sat. 9–7, Sun. 10–7; Sept.– May, Mon.–Sat. 9–5, Sun. 10–5.*

NEED A BREAK?   A traditionally Dutch way of keeping eating costs down is pancakes—laden with savory cheese and bacon, or fruit and liqueur if you have a sweet tooth. The **Pancake Bakery** (⊠ Prinsengracht 191, ☎ 020/625-1333) is one of the best places in Amsterdam to try them; the menu offers a choice of more than 30 combinations.

⓴ **Beurs van Berlage** (Berlage's Stock Exchange). Completed in 1903, the Stock Exchange is considered Amsterdam's first modern building. In 1874, when the Amsterdam Stock Exchange building on the Dam showed signs of collapse, the city authorities held a competition for the design of a new

In case you want to see the world.

At American Express, we're here to make your journey a smooth one. So we have over 1,700 travel service locations in over 120 countries ready to help. What else would you expect from the world's largest travel agency?

do more ®

http://www.americanexpress.com/travel

Travel

In case you want to be welcomed there.

We're here to see that you're always welcomed at establishments everywhere. That's why millions of people carry the American Express® Card – for peace of mind, confidence, and security, around the world or just around the corner.

do more

In case you're running low.

We're here to help with more than 118,000 Express Cash locations around the world. In order to enroll, just call American Express before you start your vacation.

do more

Express Cash

And just in case.

We're here with American Express® Travelers Cheques and Cheques *for Two*.® They're the safest way to carry money on your vacation and the surest way to get a refund, practically anywhere, anytime.
Another way we help you...

do more.

AMERICAN EXPRESS

Travelers Cheques

one. The architect who won was discovered to have copied the facade of a French town hall, so he was disqualified and the commission was awarded to a local architect, H. P. Berlage. The building that Berlage came up with proved to be an architectural turning point. Gone are all the fripperies and ornamentations of the 19th-century "neo" styles. The new Beurs, with its simple lines, earned Berlage the reputation of being the "Father of Modern Dutch Architecture." Today it serves as a concert and exhibition hall. The small museum has exhibits about the former stock exchange and its architect, as well as access to the tower. ⊠ *Damrak 213–277,* ☎ *020/626–8936.* ◻ *Fl 6.* ☉ *Tue.–Sun. 10–4.*

㊲ Brouwersgracht (Brewers Canal). The pretty, tree-lined canal is bordered by residences and former warehouses of the brewers who traded here in earlier centuries. It is blessed with long views down the main canals and plenty of sunlight, all of which makes the Brouwersgracht one of the most photographed spots in town. The canal runs westward from the end of the Singel (a short walk along Prins Hendrikkade from Centraal Station).

㊳ Centraal Station (Central Station). Designed by P. J. H. Cuypers, the architect of Amsterdam's other imposing gateway, the Rijksmuseum, this building is a landmark of Dutch neo-Renaissance style (and does bear a distinct resemblance to the museum on the other side of town). It opened in 1885 and has been the hub of transportation for the Netherlands ever since. From time to time the sumptuous **Koninklijle Wachtkamer** (Royal Waiting Room) on Platform 2 is opened to the public—and is certainly worth a visit. ⊠ *Stationsplein,* ☎ *0900/9292 (public transport information).*

㊴ Damrak (Dam Port). This busy street leading up to Centraal Station is now lined with a curious assortment of shops, attractions, hotels, and eating places. It was once a harbor bustling with activity, its piers loaded with fish and other cargo on their way to the weigh house at the Dam. During the 19th century it was filled in, and the only water that remains is a patch in front of the station that provides mooring for canal tour boats.

★ **㉜ Het Koninklijk Paleis te Amsterdam** (Royal Palace, Amsterdam). Built in the mid-17th century as the city's town hall, the Koninklijk Paleis stands solidly on 13,659 pilings sunk deep into the marshy soil of the former riverbed. Designed by Jacob van Campen, one of the most prominent architects of the time, the Stadhuis (City Hall) is a high point of the Dutch Classicist style. Inside and out, the building is adorned with rich carvings. The prosperous burghers of the Golden Age wanted a city hall that could boast of their status to all visitors—and indeed, the Amsterdam Stadhuis became known as "the Eighth Wonder of the World." When you walk into what was originally the public entrance hall, the earth is quite literally at your feet. Two maps inlaid in the marble floor show Amsterdam not just at the center of the world, but of the universe as well.

During the French occupation of the Netherlands, Louis Napoléon, who had been installed as king in 1808, decided that this was the building most suitable for a royal palace. It has been the official residence of the House of Orange ever since. Louis filled his new palace with fashionable French Empire furniture, much of which remains.

Queen Beatrix, like her mother and grandmother before her, prefers to live in the quieter environment of a palace in a park outside The Hague and uses her Amsterdam residence only on the highest of state occasions. So, once again, the former Stadhuis is open to the public. ✉ *Dam,* ☎ *020/624–8698.* 🎟 *Fl 7.* 🕐 *Oct.–May, Tues.–Thurs. 1–4; June–Sept., daily 12:30–5; occasionally closed for state events.*

★ ㊱ **Jordaan.** The renovation generation has helped make the Jordaan (pronounced yohr-dahn)—Amsterdam's Greenwich Village—the winner in the revival-of-the-fittest sweepstakes. In the western part of town, it is one of the most charming neighborhoods in a city that defines charm, basking in centuries-old patina and yet address to chic eateries and boutiques. It was originally called *jardin,* French for "garden." During the French occupation of Amsterdam, the vegetable gardens to the west of the city center were developed as a residential area. The new city quarter was referred to as the jardin, and the streets and canals (which follow the lines of the original irrigation ditches) were named for flowers and trees. In the mouths of the local Dutch, *jardin* became Jordaan, the name by which the quarter is known today.

The Jordaan was a working-class area and the scene of odorous industries, such as tanning and brewing. Its inhabitants developed a reputation for rebelliousness, but their strong community spirit also gave them a special identity, rather like London's Cockneys. Until a generation ago, native Jordaaners would call their elders "uncle" or "aunt"—and they still have a reputation for enjoying a rousing sing-a-long.

Since the 1980s, the Jordaan has gone upmarket, and now it is one of the trendiest parts of town. The narrow alleys and leafy canals are lined with quirky specialty shops, good restaurants, and designer boutiques. Students, artists, and the fashionable fill the cafés. But many of the old Jordaaners are still here—as the sound of jolly singing emanating from some local pubs will testify. The Jordaan is bounded by the Prinsengracht, Looiersgracht, Lijnbaansgracht, and Brouwersgracht canals. After a visit to the Anne Frank House, you could cross the bridge to Egelantiersgracht, the canal that runs through the heart of the Jordaan. Then zigzag through pretty side streets, such as 3e (Derde) Egelantiersdwarsstraat, Tuinstraat, and 1e (Eerste) Tuindwarsstraat, for coffee on the Noordermarkt (Northern Market). Weave back south along alleys you haven't explored yet to the antiques markets on Looiersgracht.

㉝ Nieuwe Kerk (New Church). Begun in the 14th century, the Nieuwe Kerk is a soaring Gothic structure that was never given its spire because the authorities ran out of money. Inside are the graves of the poet Vondel (known as the "Dutch Shakespeare") and Admiral Ruyter, who sailed his invading fleet up the river Medway in England in the 17th century, becoming a naval hero in the process. This church is where the inauguration ceremony has been held for every monarch since 1815. In between times it serves as a venue for special exhibitions, including the annual World Press Photo exhibition. ✉ *Dam,* ☎ *020/626–8168.* 💳 *Admission varies according to exhibition.* ☉ *Daily 11–5.*

㉞ Westerkerk (Western Church). Built between 1602 and 1631, the Westerkerk has a tower topped by a copy of the crown of the Habsburg emperor, Maximilian I. Maximilian gave Amsterdam the right to use his royal insignia in gratitude for help from the city in his struggle for control of the Low Countries. The tower, with its gaudy yellow crown, is an Amsterdam landmark. Its carillon is the comforting "clock" of the canal area of Amsterdam, and its chimes were often mentioned in the diary of Anne Frank, who was hiding just around the corner. Rembrandt and his son Titus are buried here; the philosopher René Descartes lived on the square facing the church. ⊠ *Prinsengracht (corner of Westermarkt),* ☎ *020/624–7766.* ☉ *Tower: June–Sept., Tues.–Wed. and Fri.–Sat. 2–5.*

3 Dining

AMSTERDAMMERS ENJOY GOOD FOOD, particularly when it's shared with good company. In couples or small groups, they seek out the quieter, cozy places or go in search of the new culinary stars of the city; to celebrate or entertain, they return to the institutions that never disappoint them with the quality of their cuisine or service; and in large groups, you invariably find the Dutch trooping into their favorite Indonesian restaurant to share a rijsttafel. The city's more than 700 restaurants span a wide variety of ethnic cuisines; you'll find everything from international fast-food joints to chandeliered, waterfront dining rooms frequented by the royal family. In between are small, chef-owned establishments on the canals and their side streets, restaurants that have stood the test of time on the basis of service, ambience, and consistency.

CATEGORY	AMSTERDAM*	OTHER CITIES*
$$$$	over Fl 85	over Fl 65
$$$	Fl 60–Fl 85	Fl 45–Fl 65
$$	Fl 35–Fl 60	Fl 30–Fl 45
$	under Fl 35	under Fl 30

per person for three- or four-course meal, including service and taxes and excluding drinks

Dining

$$$$ ✕ **Beddington's.** Near the Concertgebouw and the art museums, Beddington's sits at the junction between the business district and the city's most prestigious modern residential neighborhoods. The decor is ultra–minimal, designed by artist Boris Sipek. The English chef, Jean Beddington, takes an imaginative multicultural approach in the kitchen, mixing Japanese and other East Asian flavors and concepts with those from England, Spain, and the West Indies. The main courses you might encounter here are bisque of clams and lobster or perfectly balanced spring lamb with thyme. ⊠ *Roelof Hartstraat 6–8,* ☎ *020/676–5201. Reservations essential. Jacket required. AE, DC, MC, V. Closed Sun., closed lunch Sat.–Mon.*

$$$$ ✕ **De Kersentuin.** The name of this cheerful, high-ceiling restaurant, which means "cherry orchard," signals the color scheme that extends from the dinnerware to the decor. It is a good place for a leisurely meal. Although there are large windows overlooking a residential street, the focal point is the kitchen, open behind glass panels. As you dine, you can watch chef Rudolf Bos and his staff prepare French dishes with a Far Eastern twist, such as perch flavored with coconut and spicy Thai sauce, or calves' sweetbreads marinated in soy sauce and ginger. ⊠ *Dijsselhofplantsoen 7,* ☎ *020/664–2121. Reservations essential. Jacket and tie. AE, DC, MC, V. Closed Sun. No lunch.*

$$$$ ✕ **Excelsior.** The Excelsior's view over the Amstel River, to
★ the Muntplein on one side and the Music Theater on the other, is the best in Amsterdam. The dining room is a gracious, chandeliered hall with plenty of room for diners, waiters, dessert trolleys, preparation carts, towering palms, tall candelabra, and a grand piano. The approach is traditional French with a twist: You might choose a lobster bisque or an adventurous dish such as grilled turbot with shrimp and parmesan risotto. For dessert, try the delicious lemon tart or poached figs. There are five fixed-price menus. ⊠ *Hotel de L'Europe, Nieuwe Doelenstraat 2–8,* ☎ *020/531–1777. Jacket and tie. AE, DC, MC, V. No lunch Sat.*

$$$$ ✕ **'t Swarte Schaep.** This cozy upstairs restaurant over-
★ looking the noisy Leidseplein is named for a legendary black sheep that roamed the area in the 17th century. It's a study in traditional Dutch decor, with copper pots hanging from the wooden beams and heavily framed paintings on the walls. Together with this Old Holland atmosphere, the excellent French cuisine—which includes chateaubriand with béarnaise sauce and lobster mousse with asparagus salad—sometimes attracts members of the Dutch royal family during their incognito visits to the capital. Dinner orders are accepted until 11—late even for Amsterdam. ⊠ *Korte Leidsedwarsstraat 24,* ☎ *020/622–3021. Reservations essential. AE, DC, MC, V.*

$$$– ✕ **Le Garage.** On April 1, 1990, a backstreet garage near
$$$$ the Concertgebouw began a new lease on life. Oil stains and engine parts had given way to mirrored walls, plush seating, and clinking cutlery. Chef Joop Braakhekke, who is famed in the Netherlands as the zany presenter of a TV cooking show, comes up with superb New Dutch cuisine, including a few old family recipes, such as eel stewed with

32

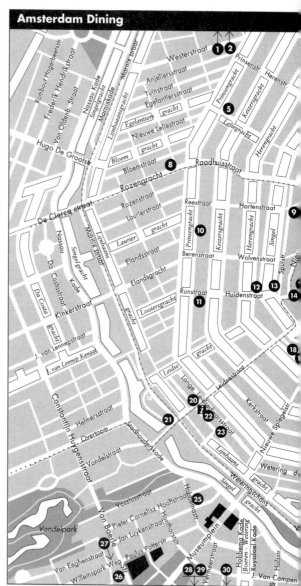
Amsterdam Dining

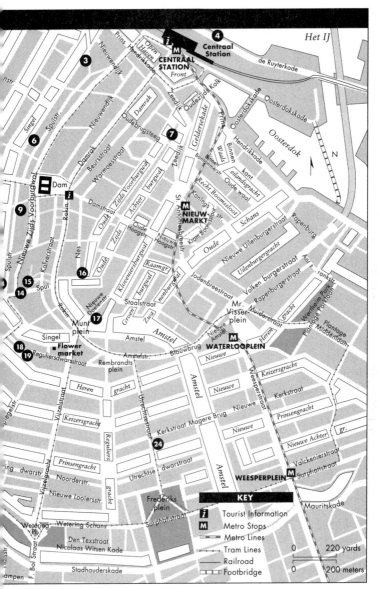

Het IJ

❹ Centraal Station

de Ruyterkade

Oosterdokskade

Oosterdok

CENTRAAL STATION *Front*

❸

Prins Hendrikkade

Open Haven Front

Zeedijk

Oudezijds Kolk

❼

Gelderskade

Hendrikkade

Binnen Waals

Binnen Bantammerstr

kant eilandsgracht

Oude waal

Oosterdokskade

N

❻

Singel

Spuistr.

Nieuwendijk

Damrak

Beursstraat

Wormoesstraat

Oudebrugsteeg

Damrak

Zeedijk

St. Anthoniebreestr.

Rechr Boomssloot

Konings

Schans

Rapenburg

Dam

❾

Nieuwe Zijds Voorburgwal

Rokin

Damstraat

Oude Zijds Voorburgwal

Achter burgwal

Oude Hoogstr

Zeids Hoogstr

Kram Boomsstoot str

M NIEUWMARKT

Oude

Nieuwe Uilenburgerstraat

Uilenburgergracht

Valken burgerstraat

Rapenburgerstraat

Anne frankstr

Spuistr.

Kalverstraat

Nes

Oude

Raamgr

Klovenierburgwal

Nieuwe nenburgwal

Jodenbreestraat

Mr. Visserplein

Muiderstraat

Henengracht

Wertheim Park

Plantage Parklaan

Plantage Middenlaan

❶❻

❶❺

❶❹

Spui

Nieuwe Doelenstr.

Staalstraat

Groenburgwal

Zwa

Munt plein

Amstel

Amstel

M WATERLOOPLEIN

Nieuwe

Amstel

Heren gracht

❶❼

❶❽

❶❾

Singel

Flower market

Reguliersdwarsstraat

Amstelstr.

Rembrandts plein

Blauwbrug

Nieuwe

Nieuwe

Nieuwe

Nieuwe Weesperstraat

Keizersgracht

Kerkstraat

Prinsengracht

Nieuwe Achter gr.

Valckenierstraat

Vijzelstraat

Heren gracht

Keizersgracht

Reguliers gracht

Prinsengracht

Utrechtsestraat

Kerkstraat Magere Brug

Amstel

❷❹

WEESPERPLEIN M

Sarphatistraat

Mauritskade

Spiegelstr.

Vijzelgracht

Noorderstr.

Nieuwe tooiersstr.

Utrechtse dwarsstraat

Frederiks plein

ing dwarstr

Wetering dwarstr.

Wetering Schans

Wetering Pl.

F. Bol Straat

ampen

Den Texstraat

Nicolaas Witsen Kade

Stadhouderskade

Sarphatistraat

KEY

𝑖 Tourist Information

M Metro Stops

━━ Metro Lines

┅┈┅ Tram Lines

━━ Railroad

▢▢▢ Footbridge

0   220 yards

0   200 meters

raisins, barley, and herbs. Media stars, politicians, and leading lights in the Dutch art world eat here, making this a hot spot for celebrity-spotters. ⊠ *Ruysdaelstraat 54,* ☎ *020/679–7176. Reservations essential. Jacket and tie. AE, DC, MC, V.*

$$$ ✕ **Café Americain.** Though thousands of buildings in Amsterdam are designated as historic monuments, the one ★ that houses this restaurant is the only structure whose interior, an Art Nouveau treasure designed by Kromhout, is also protected. Opened in 1902 and said to have been the venue for Mata Hari's wedding reception, the Café Americain is a hybrid restaurant-café serving everything from light snacks to full dinners. To one side are formal tables draped with white linens, where traditional entrées such as medallions of beef with béarnaise sauce are served; to the other side are tiny bare-top tables, perfect for a quick coffee and pastry. There is a well-stocked buffet complete with hot dishes, salads, and desserts. ⊠ *American Hotel, Leidsekade 97,* ☎ *020/624–5322. Reservations not accepted. AE, DC, MC, V.*

$$$ ✕ **Christophe.** After Algerian-born Christophe Royer opened his *eet tempel* (eating temple) on a small canal between the Keizersgracht and Prinsengracht in the 1980s, he and his French kitchen staff quickly became recognized for their fine French cuisine with Arabic and African influences. The ever-changing menu may include *crevettes à l'orange* (shrimp with orange sauce) or *pigeon à la marocaine* (pigeon cooked with coriander and other tangy spices); there is also a selection of vegetarian dishes, including a delicious artichoke with cumin. Not only is the menu special, but so are Christophe's welcoming atmosphere and personalized service. ⊠ *Leliegracht 46,* ☎ *020/625–0807. Reservations essential. Jacket advised. AE, DC, MC, V. Closed Sun., Mon., lunch; 1st wk in Jan. and 2 wks in July–Aug.*

$$$ ✕ **De Silveren Spieghel.** This intimate restaurant is in a delightfully crooked 17th-century house. The cuisine is French-★ influenced but uses the best of local ingredients, including lamb from the island of Texel and the honey of Amsterdam's Vondelpark. The seasonal game dishes are always worth trying, especially those that come with rose-petal sauce, and the fixed-price menus represent excellent value for the money. ⊠ *Kattengat 4–6,* ☎ *020/624–6589. Reser-*

vations essential. *AE, MC, V. Closed Sun. Lunch by appointment (phone a day ahead).*

$$$ ✕ **D'Vijff Vlieghen.** Dining in a traditional canal-house environment is part of the Amsterdam experience, though you are more likely to find yourself seated among closely packed tables of Swedes and Japanese than among Dutch diners. But don't let that stop you; the "Five Flies" is a charming spot that in the 1950s and 1960s was frequented by the likes of Walt Disney and Orson Welles. Set in five adjoining houses that date from 1627, the restaurant incorporates a series of small, timbered dining rooms, each well adorned with mementoes and bric-a-brac, ranging from music boxes, liqueur kegs, and violin cases to two etchings by Rembrandt. The kitchen, long a bastion of traditional Dutch meat-and-potatoes cooking, is now drawing on fresh local ingredients in such dishes as suckling pig cutlets coated in pastry, and grilled halibut with a mussel ragout. ✉ *Spuistraat 294–302,* ☎ *020/624–8369. Jacket and tie. AE, DC, MC, V.*

$$$ ✕ **Dynasty.** At this trendy, interesting spot, the decor is a fanciful mating of Asian and Art Deco. A mural in red, white, and black encircles the room, and dozens of amber and dovegray Chinese paper umbrellas hang upended from the ceiling. Chef K.Y. Lee's menu is as fascinating as the decor: The medley of Asian cuisines includes authentically prepared, classic Chinese dishes, such as Three Meats in Harmony, and selections from the cuisines of Thailand, Malaysia, and Vietnam, such as succulent duck and lobster on a bed of watercress. There are two fixed-price menus. ✉ *Reguliersdwarsstraat 30,* ☎ *020/626–8400. Jacket required. AE, DC, MC, V. No lunch. Closed Tues.*

$$$ ✕ **Tout Court.** Chef John Fagel, who comes from a well-
★ known Dutch family of chefs, has stuck by his intention to serve "good food without a fuss." This comfortable, meticulously appointed restaurant is tucked away on a side street between the canals. The owner-chef mixes generous Dutch helpings with rich sauces: saddle of lamb filled with spinach, guinea fowl stuffed with mushrooms, roast brill with leeks, and a heavenly bouillabaisse. At dinner there are three set menus, including a seven-course feast. ✉ *Runstraat 13,* ☎ *020/625–8637. AE, DC, MC, V. Closed Sun.–Mon.*

$$–$$$ ✗ **De Belhamel.** A stunning Art Deco interior and a fine view down the Herengracht set the tone for a well-prepared and attentively served dinner. In winter the emphasis is on hearty game dishes such as hart with a red wine and shallot sauce. In summer you can sample lighter fare. ⊠ *Brouwersgracht 60,* ☎ *020/622–1095. AE, MC, V. No lunch.*

$$–$$$ ✗ **De Kooning van Siam.** This Thai restaurant, which is favored by the city's Thai residents, sits smack in the middle of the red-light district, but don't let that keep you away. Although the beams and wall panels are still visible in this old canal house, there is nothing Old Dutch about the furniture or the wall decorations. Food choices are somewhat limited: Selections might include very hot stir-fried beef with onion and chili peppers or a milder chicken and Chinese vegetables with coconut, curry, and basil. ⊠ *Oude Zijds Voorburgwal 42,* ☎ *020/623–7293. AE, DC, MC, V. Closed Feb.*

$$–$$$ ✗ **De Oesterbar.** "The Oyster Bar" is a local institution. It's the first place to think of when you hanker for a half-dozen oysters fresh from the Oosterschelde or the simply prepared catch of the day. The choices are straightforward: grilled, baked, or fried fish served with tartar sauce, potatoes, and salad. Live lobster is also available in season. The no-nonsense room on the main floor has a small bar at the back, with white tile walls incorporating nautical murals and a long row of eerily lighted fish tanks along one side. In the upstairs dining room, the mood is oddly bordellolike, with elaborately patterned wallpaper and an assortment of innocuous paintings on the walls. ⊠ *Leidseplein 10,* ☎ *020/ 623–2988. Reservations essential. AE, DC, MC, V.*

$$–$$$ ✗ **D' Theeboom.** The menu here offers you a royal choice of mouthwatering and original French haute cuisine for a surprisingly low price. The interior is sparsely but stylishly furnished and the atmosphere is sophisticatedly smart. This is one of the few restaurants where you can linger over a long lunch during the week. ⊠ *Singel 210,* ☎ *020/623– 8420. Reservations essential. Jacket advised. AE, DC, MC, V. Closed lunch weekends.*

$$–$$$ ✗ **Lonny's.** Lonny Gerungan offers Indonesian cuisine at its
★   best. His family have been cooks on Bali for generations, and the recipes used for the feasts in his restaurant are those that his forefathers used for royal banquets on the island.

Treat yourself to a *Selamatan Puri Gede*, more than 15 succulently spicy dishes served with rice. The waiters wear sarongs, and the restaurant is decorated with silky fabrics and colorful parasols. ⊠ *Rozengracht 46–48,* ☎ *020/623–8950. Reservations essential. AE, DC, MC, V. No lunch.*

$$–$$$ ✕ **Lucius.** The plain setting and the simple service belie the fact that this is one of the best fish restaurants in town. On the exclusively marine menu, your choices range from grilled lobster to more adventurous creations such as sea bass with buckwheat noodles and mushrooms. You can also opt to have any fish available cooked to your taste. The wine list includes a good selection from California and even a Dutch wine from Apostlehoeve in Limburg province, the country's only vineyard. ⊠ *Spuistraat 247,* ☎ *020/624–1831. Reservations essential. AE, DC, MC, V. No lunch. Closed Sun.*

$$–$$$ ✕ **Pier 10.** This intimate restaurant, perched on the end of
★ a pier behind Centraal Station, was built in the 1930s as a shipping office. Ask for a table in the tiny glass-enclosed room at the far end of the restaurant, where the water laps gently beneath the windows and the harbor lights twinkle in the distance. Owner-chef Steve Muzerie sometimes comes up with odd combinations, such as licorice mousse with a sauce made from *advocaat* (a liqueur made with beaten egg yolks, sugar, and spirit), but his culinary inventions are usually delicious. Try the goose with wild mushrooms, or a gigantic Caesar salad. ⊠ *De Ruyterkade Steiger 10,* ☎ *020/624–8276. Reservations essential. AE, MC, V.*

$$ ✕ **Bodega Keyzer.** After 85 years spent serving musicians, concert-goers, and residents of the neighborhoods surrounding the art museums and Concertgebouw, this half restaurant, half café-bodega has evolved into something as familiar and comfortable as an old shoe. You can come at almost any hour for a simple drink or a full meal. The interior is paneled with dark wood, the lights are dim, and Oriental rugs cover the tables. The menu is equally traditional—among the meat and fish selections are tournedos, schnitzel, and sole meunière—though it may also include a more adventurous *ris de veau* (veal sweetbreads) with orange and green pepper sauce or fricassee of veal with nut-basil sauce. ⊠ *Van Baerlestraat 96,* ☎ *020/671–1441. AE, DC, MC, V. Closed Sun.*

$$ ✕ **Brasserie van Baerle.** Begun as a neighborhood lunch and Sunday brunch restaurant, this bright, appealing spot with an uncomplicated European modern decor now even draws late diners who come in following performances at the nearby Concertgebouw. The chef's creativity is the main attraction. Imaginative dishes include spicy Asian salads and heavier fare, such as duck in truffle sauce. There is outdoor dining in good weather. ⊠ *Van Baerlestraat 158,* ☎ *020/679–1532. AE, DC, MC, V. Closed Sat. and Dec. 25–Jan. 2.*

$$ ✕ **Japan Inn.** This lively Japanese restaurant is a refreshing contrast to the many tourist-trap outlets around the Leidseplein. You can choose one of various menus or order single portions to create your own dinner. There are yakitori cooked meats and fish, as well as sushi and sashimi, all served with miso soup and salad. ⊠ *Leidsekruisstraat 4,* ☎ *020/620–4989. AE, DC, MC, V. No lunch.*

$$ ✕ **Kantjil en de Tijger.** This lively Indonesian restaurant is
★ a favorite with the locals and close to the bars on the Spui. The menu is based on three different rijsttafel, with an abundance of meat, fish, and vegetable dishes varying in flavor from coconut-milk sweetness to peppery hot. Alternatively you can select separate dishes to create your own feast. ⊠ *Spuistraat 291/293,* ☎ *020/620–0994. AE, DC, MC, V. No lunch.*

$$ ✕ **Rose's Cantina.** A perennial favorite of the sparkling set, this restaurant serves up spicy Tex-Mex food and lethal cocktails. The noise level can be lethal, too. Pop in for a full meal or sundowner. In summer you can sit in the gardens facing the backs of the stately mansions on the Herengracht. ⊠ *Reguliersdwarsstraat 38,* ☎ *020/625–9797. AE, DC, MC, V.*

$$ ✕ **Sama Sebo.** Come to this small, busy, and relaxed neighborhood Indonesian restaurant near the Rijksmuseum and Museumplein for a rijsttafel feast with myriad small dishes, a simple *bami goreng* (spicy fried rice with vegetables), or a lunch of *nasi goreng* (spicy fried noodles with vegetables). The colors are muted tans and browns with rush mats covering the walls. When things are busy, the restaurant can be cramped. ⊠ *P.C. Hoofstraat 27,* ☎ *020/662–8146. AE, DC, MC, V. Closed Sun.*

$$ ✕ **Sluizer.** Sluizer is really two side-by-side restaurants with a bistrolike atmosphere—one serves only meat, the other only fish. Both are simply decorated and unpretentious; both are known for good food that is prepared without a lot of fanfare or creativity; both are reasonably priced; and, not surprisingly, both are crowded every night. ⊠ *Utrechtsestraat 43–45,* ☎ *020/622–6376 (meat)* or *020/626–3557 (fish). AE, DC, MC, V.*

$$ ✕ **Toscanini.** This cavernous, noisy Italian restaurant is
★   very popular with local trendies. The food is superb, and all prepared at the last minute. You'll find pasta with game sauce, subtle fresh fish dishes, such as trout with fresh basil, and other delights, as well as such familiar favorites as a varied plate of antipasti, which is scrumptious here. ⊠ *Lindengracht 75,* ☎ *020/623–2813. Reservations essential. No credit cards. Closed Tues. No lunch.*

$$ ✕ **Van Puffelen.** This traditional restaurant and *proeverij* (tasting house) is on a quiet section of the Prinsengracht, with a terrace if weather permits. On one side is the proeverij with a large selection of traditional Dutch jenever for you to sample. The bustling popular restaurant has classic late-19th-century fittings and fills up with locals every night of the week. If it's too noisy you can escape to the more secluded and intimate mezzanine floor. Starters include goat cheese salad; the meat main course or daily special might be braised duck's breast with passion-fruit sauce. Red meat tends to be done rare, so let them know if you prefer medium to well-done. Service is alert, and there is an excellent and reasonably priced wine list. ⊠ *Prinsengracht 375–377,* ☎ *020/624–6270. Reservations essential. AE, DC, MC, V.*

$ ✕ **Caffe Esprit.** Clean-cut and popular, this restaurant has
★   tall windows that overlook the busy Spui square; the decor is simple black, white, and gray, with just a handful of small tables and a small counter to take care of overflow. The menu is contemporary American, with choices such as Surf Burger garnished with avocado and bacon or Yankee Doodle sandwich (crisp roll with pastrami, mustard, mayonnaise, and grilled paprika). Salads include Popeye's Favorite Salad—wild Italian spinach, bacon, croutons, mushrooms, and egg, with warm tarragon vinaigrette. There are also pastas, pizzas, standard sandwiches, and a children's menu.

⊠ *Spui 10,* ☎ *020/622–1967. Reservations not accepted. No credit cards. Closed Sun.*

$ ✕ **Het Gasthuys.** In this bustling restaurant near the university you'll be served handsome portions of traditional Dutch home cooking, choice cuts of meat with excellent fries, and piles of mixed salad. Sit at the bar or take a table high up in the rafters at the back. In summer you can watch the passing boats from an enchanting canal-side terrace. ⊠ *Grimburgwal 7,* ☎ *020/624–8230. No credit cards.*

$ ✕ **The Goodies.** Fresh homemade pastas, healthy salads, and tasty meat and fish are the secret of this spaghetteria's success. During the day the restaurant is a popular café serving filling sandwiches on Italian farmer's bread, plus salads and deliciously thick fruit shakes. ⊠ *Huidenstraat 9,* ☎ *020/ 625–6122. Reservations essential. AE, MC, V.*

4 Lodging

THERE ARE SOME 270 HOTELS from which to choose in Amsterdam; most are small mom-and-pop operations, best described as pensions, found along and among the canals or in residential neighborhoods beyond the center. These smaller canal-side hotels, often in historic buildings with antique furniture, capture the charm and flavor of Amsterdam. The larger hotels, including the expensive international chains, are clustered around Centraal Station, at Dam Square, and near Leidseplein. Amsterdam is a busy city; reservations are advised at any time of the year and are essential in tulip season (late March–June).

Amsterdam is a pedestrian's paradise but a driver's nightmare. Few hotels have parking lots, and cars are best abandoned in one of the city's multistory lots for the duration of your stay. Within the concentric ring of canals that surround the downtown area, the quiet museum quarter is a convenient choice, close to both the Rijksmuseum and Vondelpark. Most atmospheric is the historic canal-side neighborhood with its gabled merchants' houses. Wherever you choose, one thing is certain: Most hotels offer rooms that are spotlessly clean.

CATEGORY	AMSTERDAM*	OTHER CITIES*
$$$$	over Fl 450	over Fl 300
$$$	Fl 400–Fl 450	Fl 200–Fl 300
$$	Fl 300–Fl 400	Fl 150–Fl 200
$	under Fl 300	under Fl 150

*for double room, including tax and service

Lodging

$$$$ 🏨 **Amstel Inter-Continental Hotel.** This grand 125-year-old hotel has an interior designed in 1992 by Pierre Yves Rochon of Paris, who has created a Dutch atmosphere with a European touch. Rooms are the most spacious in the city; the decor resembles that of a gracious home, with Oriental rugs, brocade upholstery, Delft lamps, and a color scheme inspired by the warm tones of Makkum pottery. The generous staff-guest ratio and the top-notch food explain the hotel's popularity among royals and celebrities. ⊠ *Professor Tulpplein 1, 1018 GX,* ☎ *020/622–6060,* 🅵🅰🆇 *020/622–*

5808. 58 rooms, 21 suites. 2 restaurants, 2 bars, room service, in-room VCRs, indoor pool, spa, health club, laundry service and dry cleaning, business services, convention center, meeting rooms, free parking. AE, DC, MC, V.

$$$$ 🏨 **The Grand Westin Demeure Amsterdam.** The hotel's
★ city-center site has long been associated with stately lodging: It started in the 14th century as a convent, becoming a *Princenhof* (Prince's Court) in 1578. William of Orange stayed here in 1580 and, a little later, Maria de Medici. The buildings served as the Town Hall of Amsterdam from 1808 to 1988, and even Queen Beatrix's wedding was celebrated here in 1966. Today's incarnation, opened in 1992, is a deluxe hotel; contemporary guests have included Michael Jackson. There are Gobelin tapestries, Jugendstil (Art Nouveau) stained-glass windows, and, in the café, a mural that Karel Appel created early in his career to repay a debt to the city. The rooms, which vary in size, are attractively furnished in deep tones of burgundy damask and bold floral prints; the best of them overlook the garden courtyard. The kitchen of the brasserie-style restaurant, Café Roux, is supervised by the incomparable Albert Roux. ⊠ *Oudezijds Voorburgwal 197, 1012 EX,* ☎ *020/555–3111,* FAX *020/555–3222. 138 rooms, 28 suites, 11 apartments. Restaurant, bar, in-room modem lines, in-room safes, minibars, room service, indoor pool, massage, sauna, Turkish bath, baby-sitting, laundry service and dry cleaning, meeting rooms, car rental, parking (fee). AE, DC, MC, V.*

$$$$ 🏨 **Hotel de l'Europe.** Quiet, gracious, and understated in both decor and service, this hotel overlooks the Amstel River, the Muntplein, and the flower market. The rooms are furnished with reserved, Empire-style elegance: The city-side rooms are full of warm, rich colors; the riverside rooms, decorated in pastel shades and brilliant whites, have French windows to let in floods of light. The marble baths are large and luxurious. A junior suite might be a worthwhile choice here. ⊠ *Nieuwe Doelenstraat 2–8, 1012 CP,* ☎ *020/623–4836,* FAX *020/624–2962. 80 rooms, 20 suites. 2 restaurants, bar, room service, indoor pool, barbershop, beauty salon, hot tub, massage, sauna, exercise room, business services, meeting rooms, free parking. AE, DC, MC, V.*

$$$$ 🏨 **Pulitzer.** Twenty-four 17th- and 18th-century houses
★ were combined to create this hotel, which faces both the Prin-

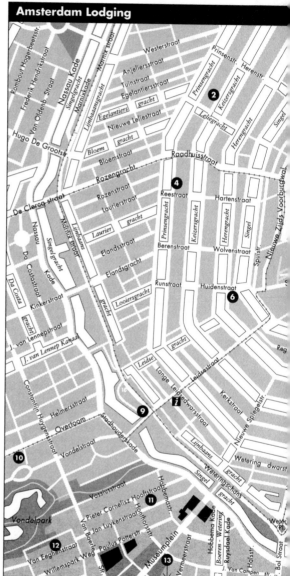

Amsterdam Lodging

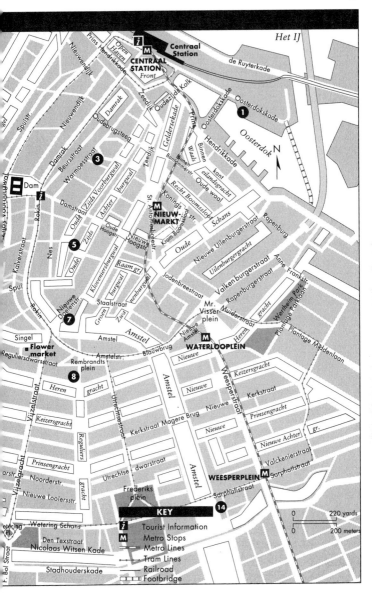

Het IJ

CENTRAAL STATION
Central Station

de Ruyterkade

Oosterdokskade

Oosterdok

1

N

Prins Hendrikkade
Open Haven
Nieuwendijk
Prins Hendrikkade
Front

Spuistr.
Damrak
Nieuwendijk
Oudebrugsteeg
Oudebrugsteeg
Leidik
Oudezijds Kolk
Geldersekade
Zeedijk

Beursstraat
Warmoesstraat
3
Damrak

Hendrikkade
Waals
Binnen
Bantammerstr.
Rommelstr.
Recht Boomssloot
kont eilandsgracht
Oude waal

Dam
Rokin
Damstraat
Oude Zijds Voorburgwal
Achter
nburgwal
St. Anthoniesdijk
Koning's
Nieuwe
Schans
NIEUW-MARKT
Kram. Koningsstr.
Rapenburg

Kalverstraat
Nes
Oude
Oude Zijds
Oude Hoogstr
Achter
Nieuwe Hoogstr
Zilds
Nieuwe Uilenburgergracht
Oude
Anne Frankstr.

Spui
Nieuwe
Raam gr.
burgwal
Klovenierschburgwal
Jodenbreestraat
Uilenburgerstraat
Valkenburgerstraat
Rapenburgerstraat
Wertheim Park
Plantage Parklaan

5
7
Nieuwe Doelenstr.
Staalstraat
Groen
Zuid
rzenburgwal
Mr. Visser-plein
Muiderstraat
gracht
Plantage Middenlaan

Singel
Flower market
Amstel
Amstel
Nieuwe Amstel
Blaauwbrug
Nieuwe Amstel
WATERLOOPLEIN
Heren
Plantage Middenlaan

Reguliersdwarsstraat
Amstelstr.
Rembrandts plein
Nieuwe
Nieuwe
Keizersgracht
Herengracht

8
Heren
gracht
Utrechtsestraat
Nieuwe
Weesperstraat
Kerkstraat

Vijzelstraat
Keizersgracht
Kerkstraat Magere Brug
Prinsengracht

Prinsengracht
Reguliers
gracht
Amstel
Nieuwe
Nieuwe Achter
gr.

Vijzelgracht
Noorderstr.
Nieuwe tooiersstr.
Utrechtse dwarsstraat
Valckenierstraat

Wetering Schans
Frederiks plein
Amstel
WEESPERPLEIN
Sarphatistraat

t. Bol Straat
Den Texstraat
Nicolaas Witsen Kade
Sarphatistraat

electing
Stadhouderskade

KEY
14

i	Tourist Information
Ⓜ	Metro Stops
—	Metro Lines
····	Tram Lines
	Railroad
▫▫▫	Footbridge

0   220 yards
0   200 meters

sengracht and the Keizersgracht canals and is just a short walk from Dam Square; the place retains a historic ambience. Most guest rooms have beam ceilings; there are gardens in the middle of the block. Refurbishment begun in 1996, while increasing comfort and convenience, is also gradually replacing modern furnishings with more appropriate antique styles. From here you may hear the hourly chiming of the Westerkerk clock. ⊠ *Prinsengracht 315–331, 1016 GZ,* ☎ *020/523–5235,* FAX *020/627–6753. 218 rooms, 7 suites, 5 apartments. 2 restaurants, bar, in-room safes, room service, pool, sauna, steam room, baby-sitting, laundry service and dry cleaning, business services, convention center, meeting rooms, parking (fee). AE, DC, MC, V.*

$$$ 🏨 **American.** The American, one of the oldest hotels in Amsterdam, is housed in one of the city's most fancifully designed buildings. Directly on Leidseplein, it's in the middle of everything—nightlife, dining, sightseeing, and shopping are all at hand. Rooms are sizable and furnished in art deco style. ⊠ *Leidseplein 28, 1017 PN,* ☎ *020/624–5322,* FAX *020/625–3236. 178 rooms, 10 suites. Restaurant, bar, room service, exercise room, shop, laundry service and dry cleaning, parking (fee). AE, DC, MC, V.*

$$ 🏨 **Ambassade.** Ten 17th- and 18th-century houses have been joined to create this hotel, which is elegantly decorated with Oriental rugs, chandeliers, and antiques. The canalside rooms are spacious, with large windows and solid, functional furniture. The rooms at the rear are quieter, but smaller and darker. Service is attentive and friendly and there are two elegant lounges. ⊠ *Herengracht 341, 1016 AZ,* ☎ *020/626–2333,* FAX *020/624–5321. 46 rooms, 5 suites, 1 apartment. Bar, in-room safes, room service, spa, baby-sitting, laundry service and dry cleaning, business services, meeting rooms, car rental, parking (fee). AE, DC, MC, V.*

$$ 🏨 **Atlas Hotel.** Just a block from Amsterdam's city-center Vondelpark, this hotel, renowned for its personal and friendly atmosphere, blends into a well-to-do residential area. The moderately sized rooms are decorated in art nouveau style. It's within easy walking distance of the museums. *Van Eeghenstraat 64, 1071 GK,* ☎ *020/676–6336,* FAX *020/671–7633. 23 rooms. Restaurant, bar, laundry service and dry cleaning, parking (fee). AE, DC, MC, V.*

$$ ⊞ **Canal House.** This is what you imagine a canal-house hotel to be like: a beautiful old home with high, plaster ceilings, antique furniture, old paintings, and a backyard garden bursting with plants and flowers. Every room is unique in both size and decor, and there isn't a television in sight. The elegant chandeliered breakfast room overlooks the garden, and there is a small bar in the front parlor. The American owners have put a lot of love and style into the Canal House—the result is an intimate hotel for adults. ⊠ *Keizersgracht 148, 1015 CX,* ☎ *020/622–5182,* 𝔉𝔞𝔵 *020/624–1317. 26 rooms. AE, DC, MC, V.*

$$ ⊞ **Jan Luyken.** This small, out-of-the-way place is barely
★ noticeable among the homes and offices of a 19th–century residential neighborhood, yet it is just one block away from the Museumplein and fashionable shopping streets. The personal approach is a relaxing alternative to the large hotels, but it is also well equipped to handle the needs of the business traveler. ⊠ *Jan Luykenstraat 58, 1071 CS,* ☎ *020/573–0730,* 𝔉𝔞𝔵 *020/676–3841. 63 rooms. Restaurant, 2 bars, in-room safes, room service, laundry service and dry cleaning, business services, parking (fee). AE, DC, MC, V.*

$–$$ ⊞ **Hotel Winston.** For the young and the young-at-heart, once a crash pad above a notorious bar, the hotel was transformed in 1996; each room has paintings or decor by a contemporary artist. It's right in the center of town, so ask for a quiet room overlooking the inner courtyard if you want to sleep before the early hours. The downstairs bar has quickly regained its reputation as a vibrant venue for live performance and late-night music; the restaurant has daily changing menus with imaginative dishes from all around the world. ⊠ *Warmoesstraat 123, 1012 JA,* ☎ *020/623–1380,* 𝔉𝔞𝔵 *020/639–2308. 66 rooms. Restaurant, bar. AE, DC, MC, V.*

$–$$ ⊞ **Seven Bridges Hotel.** This homey hotel has idyllic views of the seven canal bridges from which it took its name, but is also within a stone's throw of Rembrandtsplein. All rooms are meticulously decorated with Oriental rugs, art deco lamps, and marble sinks. Top-floor rooms are the smallest and priced accordingly; the first-floor room is practically palatial. Breakfast is delivered to your room. Reserve well in advance. ⊠ *Reguliersgracht 31, 1017 LK,* ☎ *020/623–1329. 10 rooms, 6 with shower/bath. AE, MC, V.*

$ **Amstel Botel.** This floating hotel, moored near Centraal Station, is an appropriate lodging in watery Amsterdam. The rooms are cabinlike, but the portholes have been replaced by windows that provide fine views of the city across the water. Make sure you don't get a room on the land side of the vessel, or you'll end up staring at an ugly postal sorting office. ⊠ *Oosterdokskade 2, 1011 AE,* ☎ *020/626–4247,* FAX *020/639–1952. 176 rooms. AE, DC, MC, V.*

$ **Hotel de Filosoof.** This hotel, on a quiet street near the Vondelpark, attracts artists, thinkers, and people looking for something a little different; bona fide Amsterdam philosophers are regularly to be found in the salon's comfy armchairs. Each room is decorated with a different cultural motif—there's an Aristotle room furnished in Greek style, with passages from the works of Greek philosophers hung on the walls, and a Goethe room adorned with Faustian texts. ⊠ *Anna van den Vondelstraat 6, 1054 GZ,* ☎ *020/683–3013,* FAX *020/685–3750. 29 rooms, 25 with bath. Bar. AE, MC, V.*

$ **Hotel Washington.** This small, family-run hotel is just a
★   stone's throw from the Museumplein and often attracts international musicians performing at the nearby Concertgebouw. It is simply decorated in white and pastel shades, with modern prints on the walls. Large windows let in a flood of light. The best rooms have balconies. ⊠ *F. van Mierisstraat 10, 1071 RS,* ☎ *020/679–6754,* FAX *020/673–4435. 24 rooms, 19 with shower. AE, DC, MC.*

5 Nightlife and the Arts

THE ARTS

Amsterdam's theater and music season begins in September and runs through June, when the Holland Festival of Performing Arts is held. *What's On in Amsterdam* is a comprehensive, English-language publication distributed by the tourist office that lists art and performing-arts events around the city. Reserve tickets to performances at the major theaters before your arrival through the **Netherlands Reservation Center** (⊠ Postbus 404, 2260 AK Leidschendam, ☎ 70/419–5500, FAX 070/419–5519). Tickets can also be purchased in person at the tourist information offices through the **VVV Theater Booking Office** (⊠ Stationsplein 10) Monday through Saturday, 10–4; the **AUB Ticketshop** (⊠ Leidseplein, corner Marnixstraat, ☎ 020/621–1211) Monday through Saturday, 9–9; or at theater box offices.

Film

Mainstream cinemas are concentrated near the Leidseplein; the largest is the seven-screen **City 1–7** (⊠ Kleine Gartmanplantsoen 13–25, ☎ 020/623–4579). The four-screen **Alfa 1–4** (⊠ Kleine Gartmanplantsoen 4A, ☎ 020/627–8806) shows art films and movies not on the big-time commercial circuit. Worth visiting, if only for the pleasure of sitting in its magnificent Art Deco auditorium, is the **Tuschinski** (⊠ Reguliersbreestraat 26, ☎ 020/626–2633).

Music

There are two concert halls, large and small, under one roof at the **Concertgebouw** (⊠ Concertgebouwplein 2–6, ☎ 020/671–8345). In the larger one, Amsterdam's critically acclaimed **Koninklijk Concertgebouworkest** (Royal Concert Orchestra) is often joined by international performers. The smaller hall is a venue for chamber music and up-and-coming musicians. There are free lunchtime concerts in the Concertgebouw on Wednesday at 12:30. The **IJsbreker**

(✉ Weesperzijde 23, ☎ 020/668–1805) is at the cutting edge of contemporary music and often hosts festivals of international repute.

Opera and Ballet

The grand and elegant **Muziektheater** (✉ Waterlooplein 22, ☎ 020/551 8911) seats 1,600 people and hosts international opera, ballet, and orchestra performances throughout the year. The Muziektheater is home to **De Nederlandse Opera** (The Netherlands National Opera) and **Het Nationale Ballet** (The Netherlands National Ballet). Both offer largely classical repertoires, but the dance company has, in recent years, gained a large measure of fame throughout Europe for its performances of 20th-century ballets, and the opera company is gaining international praise for its imaginative and adventurous stagings.

Puppets and Marionettes

The young and the young at heart can enjoy puppet and marionette shows at **Amsterdam Marionettetheater** (✉ Nieuwe Jonkerstraat 8, ☎ 020/620–8027).

Theater

Amsterdam's municipal theater, the **Stadsschouwburg** (✉ Leidseplein 26, ☎ 020/624–2311), mainly stages theater in Dutch but sometimes hosts smaller visiting opera companies and is beginning to turn its eye to the profitable possibilities of multicultural programming. For lavish, large-scale productions, the place to go is **Koninklijk Theater Carre** (✉ Amstel 115–125, ☎ 020/622–5225), built in the 19th century as permanent home to a circus. Amsterdam's Off-Broadway–type theaters are centered in an alley leading off the Dam and include **Frascati** (✉ Nes 63, ☎ 020/623–5723 or 020/623–5724) and **Brakke Grond** (✉ Nes 45, ☎ 020/626–6866).

NIGHTLIFE

Amsterdam nightlife centers mainly on two city squares: Leidseplein, where the cafés and discos tend to attract young visitors to the city, and Rembrandtplein, which fills up with a more local crowd. Trendier nightspots and many of Amsterdam's gay venues are on the streets in between the two squares; Reguliersdwarsstraat is a particularly happy hunting ground, while Warmoestraat and other streets in the red-light district are the scene of leather-oriented gay bars and throbbing rock clubs.

Brown Cafés

Coffee and conversation are the two main ingredients of *gezelligheid* (a good time) for an Amsterdammer, and perhaps a beer or two as the evening wears on. The best place for these pleasures is a traditional brown café. Wood paneling, wooden floors, comfortably worn furniture, and walls and ceilings stained with eons' worth of tobacco smoke give the cafés their name—though today a little carefully applied paint achieves the same effect. Traditionally, there is no background music, just the hum of chitchat. You can meet up with friends or sit alone and undisturbed for hours, enjoying a cup of coffee and a thorough read of the newspapers and magazines from the pile in the corner.

Once the tasting house of an old family distillery, **De Admiraal** (⊠ Herengracht 319, ☎ 020/625–4334) still serves potent liqueurs—many with obscene names. **De Reiger** (⊠ Nieuwe Leliestraat 34, ☎ 020/624–7426) has a distinctive Jugendstil bar and serves food. If you want to hear the locals sing folk music on Sunday afternoon, stop by **De Twee Zwaantjes** (⊠ Prinsengracht 114, ☎ 020/625–2729). A busy, jolly brown café, **In de Wildeman** (⊠ Kolksteeg 3, ☎ 020/638–2348), attracts a wide range of types and ages. **Nol** (⊠ Westerstraat 109, ☎ 020/624–5380) resonates with lusty-lunged, native Jordaaners having the time of their lives. **Rooie Nelis** (⊠ Laurierstraat 101, ☎ 020/624–4167) is one of the cafés that have kept their traditional Jordaan atmosphere despite the area's tendency toward trendiness. The high-ceiling **'t Smalle** (⊠ Egelantiersgracht 12, ☎ 020/623–9617) has a waterside terrace and is a favorite after-work gathering place.

Cabarets and Casino

Boom Chicago (⊠ Leidseplein 12, ☎ 020/530–7306) at the Leidseplein theater belongs to a bunch of zany ex-pat Americans who opened their own restaurant-theater to present improvised comedy inspired by life in Amsterdam; dinner and seating begin at 7, show time is at 8:15. **Kleine Komedie** (⊠ Amstel 56–58, ☎ 020/624–0534) has for many years been the most vibrant venue for cabaret and comedy (mainly in Dutch). One of the best additions to the nightlife scene of Amsterdam in recent years is the **Lido Dinner Show** (⊠ Leidsestraat 105, ☎ 020/626–2106), which offers cabaret and light entertainment while you dine. The **Holland Casino Amsterdam** (⊠ Max Euweplein 62, ☎ 020/620–1006), which is part of the Lido complex near Leidseplein, is one of the largest in Europe (more than 90,000 square ft) and offers everything from your choice of French or American roulette to computerized bingo, as well as the obligatory slot machines to eat up your supply of loose guilders.

Cocktail Bars

Le Bar (⊠ Hotel de l'Europe, Nieuwe Doelenstraat 2–8, ☎ 020/623–4836), cozy and stylish, is a favorite meeting place for businesspeople. **Ciel Bleu Bar** (⊠ Hotel Okura, Ferdinand Bolstraat 333, ☎ 020/678–7111) has a glass-wall lounge 23 stories high, where you can enjoy the sunsets over Amsterdam and watch the night lights twinkle to life. Comfy leather chairs and soft lighting give the **Golden Palm Bar** (⊠ Grand Hotel Krasnapolsky, Dam 9, ☎ 020/554–9111) something of the atmosphere of a British gentlemen's club.

Dance and Rock Clubs

Unabashedly commercial, **Cash** (⊠ Leidseplein 12, ☎ 020/422–0808) attracts Dutch youth from the provinces and reveling tourists. The huge, popular **Escape** (⊠ Rembrandtplein 11–15, ☎ 020/622–1111) can handle 2,500 people dancing to a DJ or live bands; attractions include laser light shows, videos, and shops selling clubwear. **iT** (✉ Amstelstraat 24, ☎ 020/625–0111), with four bars, special acts and bands, and celebrities, tends toward a gay crowd on Friday and Saturday nights, straight on Thursday and Sunday nights. If you feel like dancing in a gracious old canal house, head for **Odeon** (✉ Singel 460, ☎ 020/624–9711), where jazz and rock play in various rooms, many of which retain their spectacular painted and stucco ceilings. Converted from an old cinema, **Roxy** (✉ Singel 465, ☎ 020/620–0354) is the trendiest discotheque in the Netherlands at the moment; unless you are pretty fast-talking or smartly dressed, you may not get past the door; Wednesday is gay night. A group of artists runs **Seymour Likely Too** (✉ Nieuwezijds Voorburgwal 161, ☎ 020/420–5663), giving vent to their creativity in the decor—such as the Beuys Bar, decorated in the style of Joseph Beuys, a father of the avant-garde; sound is in the capable hands of some of Amsterdam's most popular DJs.

Gay Bars

Major newsstands carry specialized publications that include ads and listings for entertainment possibilities oriented to the interests of gays and lesbians. The gay scene in Amsterdam is concentrated mostly on Warmoesstraat, Reguliersdwarsstraat, Amstelstraat and along the Amstel, and Kerkstraat near Leidseplein. The **Gay & Lesbian Switchboard** (☎ 020/623–6565) can provide information from 10 AM to 10 PM, as can the **COC** action group (✉ Rozenstraat 14, ☎ 020/626–3087), which also operates as a coffee shop, youth café, and dance club.

Tankards and brass pots hang from the ceiling in the **Amstel Taveerne** (✉ Amstel 54, ☎ 020/623–4254), and the friendly crowd of Amsterdammers around the bar bursts into song whenever the sound system plays an old favorite. **April's Exit** (✉ Reguliersdwarsstraat 42, ☎ 020/625–8788) attracts a smart young crowd of gay men. **Downtown** (✉ Reguliersdwarsstraat 31, ☎ 020/622–9958) is a pleasant daytime coffee bar with a sunny terrace. **Le Montmartre** (✉

Halvemaansteeg 17, ☎ 020/620–7622) attracts a hip crowd of younger gay men, who stop for a drink before heading out clubbing. Amsterdam's best women-only bar, **Saarein** (✉ Elandsstraat 119, ☎ 020/623–4901) has a cozy brown-café atmosphere.

Jazz Clubs

In the smoky, jam-packed atmosphere of **Alto** (✉ Korte Leidsedwarsstraat 115, ☎ 020/626–3249), you can hear the pick of local bands. **Bamboo Bar** (✉ Lange Leidsedwarsstraat 64, ☎ 020/624–3993) has a long bar and cool Latin sounds. At **Bimhuis** (✉ Oude Schans 73–77, ☎ 020/623–3373), the best-known jazz place in town, you'll find top musicians, including avant-gardists, performing on Friday and Saturday nights, and weeknight jam sessions. **Bourbon Street Jazz & Blues Club** (✉ Leidsekruisstraat 6–8, ☎ 020/623–3440) presents mainstream blues and jazz to a largely tourist clientele. **Joseph Lam** (✉ Van Diemenstraat 242, ☎ 020/622–8086) specializes in Dixieland and is open only on Saturday.

Multicultural Performances

Akhnaton (✉ Nieuwezijdskolk 25, ☎ 020/624–3396) is a multicultural stage and dance club renowned for its world music. African nights are especially good, but there's lots of salsa and jazz, too, and even hip-hop. **De Melkweg** (The Milky Way; ✉ Lijnbaansgracht 234A, ☎ 020/624–1777 or 020/624–8492) is internationally known as a multicultural center for music, theater, film, and dance, with live music performances at least four nights a week and an innovative programming policy that tends increasingly toward multimedia events. **Paradiso** (✉ Weteringschans 6, ☎ 020/623–7348), a former church, reverberates nightly to unusual sounds—anything from the latest rock band to a serious contemporary composer. Flexible staging arrangements make this a favorite venue for performance artists and multimedia events.

6 Shopping

BONUS MILES MAKE GREAT SOUVENIRS.

MCI · Calling Card
123 456 7891 2345
J. D. SMITH
WorldPhone

Earn Miles With Your MCI Card.

Take the MCI Card along on this trip and start earning miles for the next one. You'll earn frequent flyer miles on all your calls and save with the low rates you've come to expect from MCI. Before you know it, you'll be on your way to some other international destination.

Sign up for MCI by calling
1-800-FLY-FREE

Earn Frequent Flyer Miles.

AmericanAirlines
AAdvantage®

Continental Airlines
OnePass

△ Delta Air Lines
SkyMiles®

NORTHWEST AIRLINES
WORLDPERKS®

MILEAGE PLUS.
United Airlines

US AIRWAYS
DIVIDEND MILES

Is this a great time, or what? :-)

MCI

Easy To Call Home.

1. To use your MCI Card, just dial the WorldPhone access number of the country you're calling from.
2. Dial or give the operator your MCI Card number.
3. Dial or give the number you're calling.

# Austria (CC) ♦	022-903-012
# Belarus (CC)	
From Brest, Vitebsk, Grodno, Minsk	8-800-103
From Gomel and Mogilev regions	8-10-800-103
# Belgium (CC) ♦	0800-10012
# Bulgaria	00800-0001
# Croatia (CC) ★	0800-22-0112
# Czech Republic (CC) ♦	00-42-000112
# Denmark (CC) ♦	8001-0022
# Finland (CC) ♦	08001-102-80
# France (CC) ♦	0-800-99-0019
# Germany (CC)	0800-888-8000
# Greece (CC) ♦	00-800-1211
# Hungary (CC) ♦	00▼800-01411
# Iceland (CC) ♦	800-9002
# Ireland (CC)	1-800-55-1001
# Italy (CC) ♦	172-1022
# Kazakhstan (CC)	8-800-131-4321
# Liechtenstein (CC) ♦	0800-89-0222
# Luxembourg	0800-0112
# Monaco (CC) ♦	800-90-019
# Netherlands (CC) ♦	0800-022-9122
# Norway (CC) ♦	800-19912
# Poland (CC) ÷	00-800-111-21-22
# Portugal (CC) ÷	05-017-1234
Romania (CC) ÷	01-800-1800
# Russia (CC) ÷ ♦	
To call using ROSTELCOM ■	747-3322
For a Russian-speaking operator	747-3320
To call using SOVINTEL ■	960-2222
# San Marino (CC) ♦	172-1022
# Slovak Republic (CC)	00-421-00112
# Slovenia	080-8808
# Spain (CC)	900-99-0014
# Sweden (CC) ♦	020-795-922
# Switzerland (CC) ♦	0800-89-0222
# Turkey (CC) ♦	00-8001-1177
# Ukraine (CC) ÷	8▼10-013
# United Kingdom (CC)	
To call using BT ■	0800-89-0222
To call using C&W ■	0500-89-0222
# Vatican City (CC)	172-1022

Flying to France on
Friday? Get Francs
from Chase on
Thursday. Call
Currency To Go at
935-9935 for
overnight delivery.

Or pounds for London. Or Deutschmarks for Düsseldorf. Or any
of 75 foreign currencies. Call **Chase Currency To Go**^{SM} at **935-9935**
in area codes 212, 718, 914, 516 and Rochester, N.Y.; all other area
codes call 1-800-935-9935. We'll deliver directly to your door.*
Overnight. And there are no exchange fees. Let Chase make your
trip an easier one.

CHASE. The right relationship is everything.^{SM}

THE VARIETY OF GOODS available here and the convenience of a shopping district that snakes through the city in a continuous parade of boutiques and department stores are the major joys of shopping in Amsterdam. Be sure to visit the year-round outdoor flea market at Waterlooplein, a holdover from the pushcart days in the Jewish Quarter. Shopping hours in the Netherlands are regulated by law: One night a week is reserved for late shopping. In Amsterdam, department stores and many other shops are closed Monday morning but open Thursday evening. Increasingly, following an easing of legislation governing shopping hours, you'll find main branches of major stores in the center of the city open on Sunday afternoon.

Shopping Districts and Streets

The **Dam Square** is home to two of Amsterdam's main department stores. Several popular shopping streets radiate from the square, offering something for nearly all tastes. **Kalverstraat,** the city's main pedestrians-only shopping street, is where Amsterdam does its day-to-day shopping. The imposing new **Kalvertoren** shopping mall (⊠ Kalverstraat, near Munt), offers covered shopping and a rooftop restaurant with magnificent views of the city. **Leidsestraat** offers a range and variety of shopping similar to Kalverstraat's, but with more of an eye to the tourist trade. **Max Euweplein** is a small plaza-style shopping mall surrounding a summer café and adjacent to the Amsterdam Casino. **Nieuwendijk** is a busy pedestrian mall, good for bargain hunters. The **Magna Plaza** shopping center (⊠ Nieuwezijds Voorburgwal 182), built inside the glorious old post office behind the Royal Palace, is *the* place for A-to-Z shopping in a huge variety of stores. The posh and prestigious **P.C. Hooftstraat,** generally known as the P.C. (pronounced "pay-say"), is home to chic designer boutiques; this is where diplomats and politicians buy their glad rags. **Rokin** is the place to go for high-price fashion and jewelry, Old Masters, and expensive antiques. **Utrechtsestraat** offers a variety of opportunities for the trendier shopper. **Van Baerlestraat,** leading to the Concertgebouw, is lined with clothing shops that are smart—but not quite smart enough to have made it to the adjoining P.C. Hooftstraat.

Department Stores

C&A (⊠ Damrak 79, ☎ 020/626–3132) offers discount clothing. **De Bijenkorf** (⊠ Dam 1, ☎ 020/621–8080) is the city's best-known department store and the stomping ground of its monied middle classes. The gracious and conservative **Maison de Bonneterie en Pander** (⊠ Rokin 140–142, ☎ 020/626–2162), all crystal chandeliers and silently gliding shop assistants, stocks an elegant range of clothing and household items. The Amsterdam branch of England's **Marks & Spencer** (⊠ Kalverstraat 66–72, ☎ 020/620–0006) is a good bet for inexpensive clothing and expensive food. **Metz & Company** (⊠ Keizersgracht 455, ☎ 020/624–8810) stocks up on textiles and household goods from **Liberty of London** and adds a range of breathtakingly expensive designer articles from all over the world; at the top-floor café you can get the best bird's-eye view of the city. **Peek & Cloppenburg** (⊠ Dam 20, ☎ 020/622–8837) specializes in durable, middle-of-the-road clothing. **Vroom & Dreesmann** (⊠ Kalverstraat 203, ☎ 020/622–0171), Amsterdam's third smartest department store after De Bijenkorf and Maison de Bonneterie, sells good-quality clothing.

Street Markets

Few markets compare with Amsterdam's **Waterlooplein** flea market. It is a descendant of the haphazard pushcart trade that gave this part of the city its distinct and lively character in the early part of the century. You're unlikely to find anything of value here, but it's a good spot to look for the secondhand clothing young Amsterdammers favor, and it is a gadget lover's paradise. The flea market is open Monday through Saturday 9:30–5. The **Bloemenmarkt** (along the Singel canal, between Koningsplein and Muntplein) is another of Amsterdam's must-see markets, where flowers and plants are sold from permanently moored barges. The market is open Monday through Saturday 9:30–6 (some flower stalls are open Sunday). On Saturday, the Noordermarkt and Nieuwmarkt host an **organic farmers' market,** with specialist stalls selling essential oils and other New Age fare alongside the oats, pulses, and vegetables. **Sunday art markets** are held in good weather from April to October on Thorbeckeplein, and from April through November at Spui. The **Postzegelmarkt** stamp market is held twice a week (Wednesday and Saturday 1–4) on Nieuwezijds Voorburgwal.

Specialty Stores

Antiques

Antiques always have been a staple item of shopping in Amsterdam, and the array of goods available at any time is broad. There are more than 150 antiques shops scattered throughout the central canal area. The greatest concentration of those offering fine antiques and specialty items is in the **Spiegel Quarter.** Nieuwe Spiegelstraat and its continuation, **Spiegelgracht,** constitute the main thoroughfare of the quarter, with shops on both sides of the street and canal for five blocks, from the Golden Bend of the Herengracht nearly to the Rijksmuseum, including several dealers under one roof in the **Amsterdam Antiques Gallery** (✉ Nieuwe Spiegelstraat 34, ☎ 020/625–3371). For a broad range of vintage and antique furniture, curios, jewelry, clothing, and household items, try **Kunst- & Antiekmarkt De Looier** (✉ Elandsgracht 109, ☎ 020/624–9038), an art and antiques market housing more than 50 dealers. The indoor flea market, **De Rommelmarkt** (✉ Looiersgracht 38, ☎ 020/627–4762), is a warren of stalls selling everything from Art Deco lamps to defunct electrical equipment. Rokin, between Dam and Muntplein, is the location of the Amsterdam branch of **Sotheby's** (✉ Rokin 102, ☎ 020/550–2200). A number of the sorts of art and antiques stores where museum curators do their shopping, including **Waterman** (✉ Rokin 116, ☎ 020/623–2958), are on Rokin. Shops on **Rozengracht** and **Prinsengracht,** near the Westerkerk, offer country Dutch furniture and household items; you'll also find antiques and curio shops along the side streets in that part of the city.

There are old maps and prints (including botanicals) in antiques shops all over Amsterdam, but for a broad selection of high quality, visit **A. van der Meer** (✉ P.C. Hooftstraat

112, ☏ 020/662–1936), a gallery that has specialized in 17th-, 18th-, and 19th-century works for more than 30 years. Daumier etchings, hunt prints, and cityscape engravings can also be found here. **De Haas** (✉ Kerkstraat 155, ☏ 020/626–5952) specializes in smaller pieces from the beginning of the 20th century. **Galerie Frans Leidelmeyer** (✉ Nieuwe Spiegelstraat 58, ☏ 020/625–4627) is a good source of top-quality Art Deco and Jugendstil artifacts. **Tangram** (✉ Herenstraat 9, ☏ 020/624–4286) deals in the Art Deco and Jugendstil items that are so popular in the Netherlands.

Art

Many of the galleries that deal in modern and contemporary art are centered on the **Keizersgracht** and **Spiegel Quarter.** *What's On in Amsterdam,* published by the tourist office, is a good source of information on current exhibitions; another is the Dutch-language publication *Alert,* which has the most comprehensive listings available. Among the dealers specializing in 20th-century art along the Keizersgracht are **D'Art 1970** (✉ Keizersgracht 516, ☏ 020/622–1511), **Galerie Espace** (✉ Keizersgracht 548, ☏ 020/624–0802), and **Kunsthandel M.L. De Boer** (✉ Keizersgracht 542, ☏ 020/623–4060). In the Spiegel Quarter, the leading galleries are: **C.M. Kooring Verwindt** (✉ Spiegelgracht 14–16, ☏ 020/623–6538), **E. Den Bieman de Haas** (✉ Nieuwe Spiegelstraat 44, ☏ 020/626–1012), **Galerie Asselijn** (✉ Lange Leidsedwarsstraat 200, ☏ 020/624–9030), **Galerie Guido de Spa** (✉ 2e Weteringdwarsstraat 34, ☏ 020/622–1528), **Marie-Louise Woltering** (✉ Nieuwe Spiegelstraat 53, ☏ 020/622–2240), and **Wetering Galerie** (✉ Lijnbaansgracht 288, ☏ 020/623–6189).

Couzijn Simon (✉ Prinsengracht 578, ☏ 020/624–7691) specializes in molting teddies and other vintage toys. **Eurasia Antiques** (✉ Nieuwe Spiegelstraat 40, ☏ 020/626–1594) is a treasure trove of old paintings, engravings, and Asian art. **Galerie Animation Art** (✉ Berenstraat 39, ☏ 020/627–7600) offers original Disney and other cartoon sketches.

Books

Allert de Lange (✉ Damrak 60–62, ☏ 020/624–6744) has a good selection of fiction and books on travel and history. True to its name, the **American Book Center** (✉ Kalverstraat 185, ☏ 020/625–5537) is strongly oriented to American tastes and expectations. **The English Bookshop** (⊠ Lauri-ersgracht 71, ☎ 020/626–4230) is a cozy canal-side book-shop with a good range of English literature, travel books, and magazines. **Premsela** (⊠ Van Baerlestraat 78, ☎ 020/662–4266) specializes in art books and stocks many lus-cious, tempting tomes. **Waterstone's** (⊠ Kalverstraat 152, ☎ 020/638–3821) has four floors of English-language books, from children's stories to computer manuals.

Ceramics and Crystal
Focke & Meltzer (⊠ P.C. Hooftstraat 65–67, ☎ 020/664–2311; ⊠ Hotel OOkura Shopping Arcade, ☎ 020/678–7111) is the primary source in Amsterdam of authenticated Delft and Makkumware, as well as fine crystal.

Cigars and Smoking
Davidoff (⊠ Van Baerlestraat 84, ☎ 020/671–1042) stocks fine cigars and other smokers' requisites. One of the best places in the world to buy cigars and other smoking ma-terials is **Hajenius** (⊠ Rokin 92, ☎ 020/623–7494), in busi-ness since 1826.

Coffee, Tea, and Spices
Jacob Hooy & Co. (⊠ Kloveniersburgwal 12, ☎ 020/624–3041) has been selling herbs, spices, and medicinal po-tions from the same shop beside the Nieuwmarkt since 1743. Gold-lettered wooden drawers, barrels, and bins contain not just spices and herbs but also a daunting array of *drop-jes* (hard candies and medicinal drops) and teas. **S. Levelt's Koffie-en Theehandel N.V.** (⊠ Prinsengracht 180, ☎ 020/624–0823) offers nearly 100 different kinds of tea and more than two dozen coffees.

Diamonds and Jewelry
The **Amsterdam Diamond Center** (⊠ Rokin 1–5, ☎ 020/624–5787) houses several diamond sellers. **Coster Diamonds** (⊠ Paulus Potterstraat 2–4, ☎ 020/676–2222) not only sells jewelry and loose diamonds but gives free demonstrations of diamond cutting. You can see a replica of the most famous diamond cut in the factory—the Koh-I-Noor, one of the prize gems of the British crown jewels. **Van Moppes Diamonds** (⊠ Albert Cuypstraat 2–6, ☎ 020/676–1242) has an ex-tensive diamond showroom and offers a glimpse of the pro-cess of diamond cutting and polishing.

Bonebakker (⊠ Rokin 88/90, ☎ 020/623–2294) is one of the city's oldest and finest jewelers and carries an exceptionally fine range of watches and silverware. **Premsela & Hamburger** (⊠ Rokin 120, ☎ 020/624–9688; closed weekends) has sold fine antique silver and jewelry since 1823. The century-old **Schaap and Citroen** (⊠ Kalverstraat 1, ☎ 020/626–6691) has an affordable range of jewelry and watches.

Duty-Free

If you don't have time to shop in Amsterdam, save your guilders for the airport, as **Amsterdam Airport Shopping Centre** (⊠ Amsterdam Schiphol Airport, ☎ 020/601–2497) is bigger, better, and cheaper than almost any other airport duty-free shopping area in the world. The airport's departure hall looks more like a shopping mall than a transportation facility, and auxiliary shops for the most popular items (liquor, perfume, chocolates) are found in every wing of the terminal.

Men's Clothing

For high-style apparel and designer togs, head to **Dik** (⊠ P.C. Hooftstraat 35, ☎ 020/662–4328). **The English Hatter** (⊠ Heiligeweg 40, ☎ 020/623–4781) has tweed jackets, deerstalkers, and many other trappings of the English country gentleman. **Gaudi** (⊠ P.C. Hooftstraat 116, ☎ 020/679–9319) is a mecca for the trendy and label conscious. **McGregor and Clan Shop** (⊠ P.C. Hooftstraat 113, ☎ 020/662–7425) has a distinctly Scottish air, with chunky knitwear and the odd flash of tartan. **Meddens** (⊠ Heiligeweg 11–17, ☎ 020/624–0461) stocks a good range of fairly conservative men's casual and formal wear. **Mulberry Company** (⊠ P.C. Hooftstraat 46, ☎ 020/673–8086) sells stylish fashions from England. **Oger** (⊠ P.C. Hooftstraat 81, ☎ 020/676–8695) puts suits on the backs of leading Dutch politicians and TV personalities. **Society Shop** (⊠ Van Baerlestraat 20, ☎ 020/664–9281) stocks good basics for businessmen.

Shoes and Hats

Bally Shoes (⊠ Leidsestraat 8–10, ☎ 020/622–2888) is a byword for good taste in women's shoes. **Dr. Adams** (⊠ P.C. Hooftstraat 90, ☎ 020/662–3835) sells chunkier, more adventurous styles of shoes for men and women. **Shoebaloo** (⊠ Koningsplein 7, ☎ 020/626–7993) is the place for 8-inch heels, mock leopard-skin boots, and other outrageous footwear. **Smit Bally** (⊠ Leidsestraat 41, ☎ 020/624–8862) sells classically smart shoes for men.

The well-stocked **Hoeden M/V** (⊠ 422 Herengracht, ☎ 020/626–3038), in a canal house, carries Borsalino hats for men and women as well as Dutch and international designer hats.

Women's Clothing

In the **Jordaan** neighborhood, generation after generation of experimental designers have set up shop to show their imaginative creations. Antiques- and used-clothing shops are also in this part of town. Designer shops stand shoulder to shoulder in the **P.C. Hooftstraat: Benetton** (⊠ P.C. Hooftstraat 72, ☎ 020/679–5706), **Edgar Vos** (⊠ P.C. Hooftstraat 134, ☎ 020/662–6336), **Leeser** (⊠ P.C. Hooftstraat 117, ☎ 020/679–5020), and **Max Mara** (⊠ P.C. Hooftstraat 110, ☎ 020/671–7742). **Boetiek Pauw** (⊠ Van Baerlestrasse 66 and 72, ☎ 020/662–6253), which also operates men's and children's shops, is part of a chain that stands out for the quality of both design and craftsmanship of its clothing. The international fashion house **Esprit** (⊠ Spui 1c, ☎ 020/626–3624) has a large branch in central Amsterdam. **Claudia Sträter** (⊠ Beethovenstraat 9, ☎ 020/673–6605; ⊠ Kalverstraat 179–181, ☎ 020/622–0559) is part of a Dutch minichain that sells simply styled, well-made clothes for all occasions.

7 Side Trips from Amsterdam

THE BULB FIELDS AND FLOWER AUCTION

Even if you are in Amsterdam for just a couple of days, it is easy to sample one of the best-known aspects of quintessential Holland—the bulb fields. The flower-growing area to the west of Amsterdam is a modern-day powerhouse of Dutch production techniques, which mean that you can encounter Dutch flowers all over the world at any time of the year. In spring, the bulb fields blaze with color: Great squares and oblongs of red, yellow, and white look like giant Mondrian paintings laid out on the ground. It is a spectacular sight, whether you travel through the fields by bike or bus, or pass by in the train on your way to Leiden.

Driving from Amsterdam, take the A4 southbound toward Leiden. Take the N207 turning for Lisse. The Bollenstreek Route (Bulb District Route) is a special itinerary through the heart of the flower-growing region that was laid out by the Dutch auto club, ANWB. The route is marked with small blue and white signs that read BOLLENSTREEK. It begins in Oegstgeest, near Leiden, and circles through Rijnsburg (site of one of Holland's three major flower auction houses), where there is a colorful Flower Parade on the first Saturday in August. On the way you pass through Lisse, which has a Flower Parade on the last Saturday in April. Lisse is also the site of the Keukenhof Gardens.

Numbers in the margin correspond to points of interest on the Side Trips from Amsterdam map.

Keukenhof

❶ *34 km (21 mi) southwest of Amsterdam.*

Keukenhof is a 70-acre park and greenhouse complex where nearly 7 million flowers bloom every spring. In the last weeks of April you can catch tulips, daffodils, hyacinths, and narcissi all flowering simultaneously. In addition there are bright floral mosaics and some 50,000 square ft of more exotic blooms under glass. The first tulip bulbs were brought to the Netherlands from Turkey in the mid-16th century. During the 17th century the bulbs became a

Side Trips from Amsterdam

De Koog **8** Texel

Den Burg **6** **7** Oudeschild

Den Helder

N99

N227/A7

N99

Stavoren

N248

N242

IJsselmeer

N241

Enkhuizen

5

Alkmaar

N243

4 **Hoorn**

Noordoost Polder

Urk

Castricum

Markermeer

Purmerend

Edam

Volendam

Zaandam

Marken

Monnickendam

Oostelijk Flevoland

3

Haarlem

Zandvoort

✪ Amsterdam

Zuidelijk Flevoland

Hillegom

✈ Schiphol Airport

Noordwijk

1

2 **Aalsmeer**

Apeldoorn

Katwijk

Keukenhof

E30/A1

E232/A8

N

KEY

🚂 Rail Lines

- - - Ferry

0   10 miles

0   15 km

prized possession and changed hands for extraordinary amounts of money. Today Dutch botanists use Keukenhof as a showcase for their latest hybrids, so black tulips and gaudy frilled varieties also make an appearance. ⌧ *N207, Lisse;* ☎ *0252/465–555.* 🎟 *Fl 17.50.* ☼ *Late Mar.–May, daily 8–7:30.*

After visiting Keukenhof, check out the dunes north of **Noordwijk.** You'll find a vast, sandy nature reserve, almost as big as the bulb district itself. Small canals and pools of water are dotted about in between the dunes, providing a haven for bird life. In addition to Noordwijk, the Bulb Route (☞ *above*) passes through the beach community of **Katwijk** and through **Sassenheim,** where there is an imposing 13th-century ruined castle.

Aalsmeer

2 *About 19 km (12 mi) south of Amsterdam near Schiphol Airport.*

The **Bloemenveiling Aalsmeer** (Aalsmeer Flower Auction) is held in Aalsmeer five days a week from the pre-dawn hours until mid-morning. The largest flower auction in the world, it has three auction halls operating continuously in a building the size of several football fields. You walk on a catwalk above the rolling four-tier carts that wait to move on tracks past the auctioneers. The buying system is what is called a Dutch auction—the price goes down, not up, on a large "clock" on the wall. The buyers sit lecture-style with buzzers on their desks; the first to register a bid gets the bunch. ⊠ *Legmeerdijk 313, Aalsmeer*, ☎ *0297/392–185.* 🖅 *Fl 7.* ⊙ *Weekdays 7:30–11.*

FOLKLORIC HOLLAND

Amsterdam is actually in the southern part of the province of Noord-Holland. Just across the Noordzee Kanaal (North Sea Canal) behind Amsterdam's Centraal Station as far as the Kop van Holland (the Top of Holland) and the island of Texel, this part of the country offers a taste of unspoiled rural life. Characterful towns, once home to the Dutch fishing fleets and the adventurous captains of the Dutch Golden Age who traveled to the East and West Indies and beyond, are now obsolete because of the *Afsluitdijk* (Enclosing Dike) at the north end of the former Zuider Zee. This extraordinary piece of civil engineering was completed in 1932, protecting the low-lying land from the ravages of the open seas and creating a massive freshwater lake. These ports are now busy harbors for the leisure craft that ply the protected waters, but the province's heritage has been preserved in the many museums that recall the activities of yesteryear.

Zaandam

❸ *16 km (10 mi) northwest of Amsterdam.*

The **Zaanse Schans** is a gem of windmill-studded countryside in the province of Noord Holland. It is just north of Zaandam, where Peter the Great of Russia learned the craft of shipbuilding. The village is filled with classic green wooden houses. Many have been restored as private homes, but a whole cluster is open to the public, including the workshop of a clog maker, the shops of a traditional cheese maker, a bakery museum, and the working windmills themselves. ⊠ *Kraaienest, Zaandam,* ☎ *075/616–8218.* 🎫 *Free.* ⊙ *Daily 8:30–6.*

Hoorn

❹ *43 km (27 mi) north of Amsterdam.*

The former capital of West-Friesland was an important center for the fleets of the VOC (Dutch East India Company) during the 17th century. Willem Cornelis Schouten, one of the town's sons, was the first sailor to round the southern cape of America (in 1616), and christened it Cape Hoorn. Jan Pieterszoon Coen, whose statue lords over the Rode Steen square, founded the city of Batavia in Java, the present-day Jakarta, and governed it from 1617 until his death in 1629. Hoorn's decline was precipitated by the growing naval power of the British during the 18th century and the opening of Noord-Holland's canal linking Amsterdam directly to the North Sea. Nowadays it is a leisurely yacht harbor on the enclosed IJsselmeer.

The **Westfries Museum** (West Frisian Museum) is housed in the provincial government building from 1632, where the delegates from the seven cities of West-Friesland used to meet. The cities are represented by the coats of arms decorating the stunning facade, a testimony to the province's former grandeur. The council chambers are hung with portraits of the region's grandees, and the exhibitions explain the town's maritime history and the exotic finds of its adventurous sailors. ⊠ *Rode Steen 1,* ☎ *0229/280–028.* 🎫 *Fl 6.* ⊙ *Apr.–Sept., weekdays 11–5, Sat. 2–5, Sun. noon–5; Oct.–Mar., weekdays 11–5, weekends 2–5.*

. . . .

NEED A BREAK?   **De Waag** (The Weigh House; ⊠ Rode Steen 8, ☎ 0229/215–195) is a monumental building dating from 1609, with wooden beams and the antique weighing equipment still intact. It was designed by Hendrick de Keyser. There are soups, salads, and well-filled sandwiches during the day, and at dinner time you can choose from fish specialties or French cuisine. The terrace affords a stunning view of the towering ornamental facade of the Westfries Museum across the square.

Enkhuizen

❺ *About 19 km (12 mi) east of Hoorn.*

☾ Near the former harbor town of Enkhuizen is the **Zuiderzee Museum.** It is one of the Netherlands' most complete outdoor museums, with streets, neighborhoods, and harbors created with historic buildings. There are 130 houses, shops, and workshops where old crafts are still practiced. To reach the museum you have to take a boat from the main entrance, a romantic way to take a step back in time. The children's island takes youngsters back to life in the former fishing village of Marken during the 1930s. ⊠ *Wierdijk 12–22, Enkhuizen,* ☎ *0228/351–111.* ⊠ *Fl 17.50; indoor museum only, Fl 7.50.* ☉ *Indoor museum, daily 10–5; outdoor museum, Apr.–Oct., daily 10–5.*

Texel

85 km (53 mi) north of Amsterdam.

The largest of the Wadden Islands is also the easiest to reach, just over an hour from Amsterdam by road or rail, and only 20 minutes from the mainland by ferry. With an early start you could tour it by bike in a day. Otherwise take a night or two to enjoy the nature, sea breeze, and clear skies. Texel is nicknamed "Holland in miniature" because of the variety of landscape and natural features: woodlands, open meadows, saltwater marshes, dunes, and broad beaches. The many nature reserves make it a paradise for bird-watchers. Water sports are important here, and the island's annual *Ronde om Texel,* a 100-km (60-mi) catamaran race around the island held in mid-June and preceded by a week of other maritime events, has become famous. The island also has an international sea-kayaking school, parachute jumping, and a golf course.

One of Texel's remarkable natural features is **De Hoge Berg** (the High Mountain), the 50-ft-high pinnacle of a ridge formed by glacial movement during the last Ice Age and declared a natural monument in 1968. Climbing its grass-covered pathways is hardly a problem, but it offers a stunning overview of the whole island. Throughout the island you can spot the unusual *schapeboet*, sheep shelters that look like truncated barns, some thatched with local reed, with their sloping rumps turned to the westerly winds. The characteristic *tuinwallen* (garden walls) that were used to divide plots of farmland were built up from sods of earth. These have become a habitat for all kinds of plants, animals, and insects.

❻ **Den Burg** is at the center of the island, geographically, as well as in terms of size, choice of places to eat, and shops. The step-gabled house occupied by the **Oudheidskamer** (Museum of Antiquities) dates from 1599 and gives a sense of local life in times gone by, with exquisitely tiled fireplaces and antique furniture in a homey setting. ⊠ *Kogerstraat 1,* ☎ *0222/313–135.* 🎫 *Fl 3.* ۞ *Apr.–Oct. weekdays 10–noon and 1:30–3:30.*

❼ **Oudeschild** is the island's historic harbor town, still used as a port by Texel's modern fishing fleet. During the 17th century, VOC (Dutch East India Company) ships would anchor here, awaiting favorable winds to take them off on their adventurous journeys, and smaller boats would bring them provisions. Sports fishing trips and shrimping fleets now set out from here.

The **Maritiem en Jutters Museum** (Maritime and Beachcomber's Museum) contains a bemusing collection of beachcombers' finds and is just next door to the landmark **Traanroier molen** (Tear Rower windmill), which was used for hulling grain. The museum also has exhibitions about the local fishing industry, lifeboats, and marine archaeology, including the finds from a VOC ship that sank in the Wadden Sea in 1640. ⊠ *Barentszstraat 21, Oudeschild,* ☎ *0222/314–956.* 🎫 *Fl 8.* ۞ *Sept.–June, Tues.–Sun. 10–5; July–Aug., daily 10–5.*

One of Texel's oldest constructions is **Fort De Schans.** Built in the 15th century, this fort is surrounded by water-filled moats. It was extended in 1811 on the orders of Napoléon. ⊠ *Schansweg, 1 km (½ mi) south of Oudeschild.* 🎫 *Guided tours Fl 10.* ۞ *Tours: Apr.–Oct., Wed. 10.*

8 **De Koog,** a modern seaside town, is a practical base for exploring the North Sea coastline and its nature reserves. In high season it is subject to hordes of sunseeking tourists. Much of northwestern Texel is new, the result of dikes built early in the 17th century. Sand was deposited on the seaward side of these dikes, forming a second row of dunes that protected the land behind. However, if the sea breaks through the dunes or man-made dikes during a storm, the valleys behind them can become tidal salt marshes. This is how the **De Slufter** and **De Muy** nature reserves were formed, ideal feeding and breeding grounds for birds such as the spoonbill, sandpipers, and even the rare avocet.

The **Ecomare** nature center for the Wadden Sea and the North Sea is a good starting point for discovering the natural wonders of these abundant habitats. There is a seal rehabilitation center, a bird sanctuary, and fieldwork programs for the public. ✉ *Ruyslaan 92, De Koog,* ☎ *0222/317-741.* 🎫 *Fl 12.50.* ☉ *Apr.–Oct., daily 9–5; Nov.–Mar., Mon.–Sat. 9–5.*

Dining and Lodging

Texel's sheep outnumber the human population. The lambs are famous for their succulent pre-salé saltiness, acquired from grazing in meadows sprayed by the salt-laden sea winds. The island is also known for its organic dairy products and vegetables. The salt marshes make it possible to farm unusual vegetables such as sea aster, a leaf that makes a tasty addition to salads. There is plenty of holiday accommodation on Texel, from campsites in the dunes to private villas hidden in woodlands. Contact the VVV (☞ Visitor Information, *below*) for further information; a variety of packages that can reduce hotel costs considerably are available. For price charts, *see* Chapters 3 and 4.

$$$$ ✕ **Het Vierspan.** This intimate but sophisticated restaurant serves carefully prepared Continental cuisine emphasizing the famous local products, for example a starter of carpaccio of duck's breast followed by saddle of Texel lamb. The day menu is created using only the very freshest products. ✉ *Gravenstraat 3, Den Burg,* ☎ *0222/013–176. AE, MC, V. No lunch.*

$$–$$$$ 🏨 **Hotel & Villa Opduin.** This establishment tries to uphold the values of the family hotel from which it has developed. Though architecturally the hotel is nothing short of a modern, blocklike monstrosity, the rooms are spacious and filled with light. There are a few luxury top-floor suites with a view of the sea; the hotel's dependance, Villa Opduin, has simple, cheap rooms with shared bathrooms. ⊠ *Ruyslaan 22, 1796 AD, De Koog,* ☎ *0222/317–445,* ℻ *0222/317–777. 59 rooms, 42 suites, 6 apartments. Restaurant, bar, lobby lounge, in-room safes, minibars, indoor pool, sauna, tennis court, bicycles, children's programs, convention center, meeting rooms. AE, MC, V.*

$$ 🏨 **Hotel De Lindeboom.** Spacious, light rooms with modern furnishings are above a popular café-restaurant with a sunny terrace that overlooks an open square in the peaceful center of town. ⊠ *Groeneplaats 14, 1791 CC, Den Burg,* ☎ *0222/312–041,* ℻ *0222/310–517. 22 rooms. Restaurant, bar. No credit cards.*

$ 🏨 **Hotel-Restaurant De Zeven Provinciën.** The old-fashioned tavern with simple rooms nestles safely behind the sea dike on the eastern side of the island. The restaurant serves traditional Dutch food throughout the day. ⊠ *De Ruyterstraat 60, 1792 AK, Oudeschild,* ☎ *0222/312–652. 14 rooms. Restaurant, bar. No credit cards.*

Outdoor Activities and Sports

BIKING

Bicycles can be rented from the ferry terminal and all over the island for about Fl 7.50 per day.

CATAMARAN SAILING

Training courses and rentals are available at **Zeilschool De Eilander** (⊠ Paal 33, De Cocksdorp, ☎ 0222/316–500) and **J. Schuringa** (⊠ Westerslag, Paal 15, De Koog, ☎ 0222/314–847).

GOLF

The island's golf course and driving range is **De Texelse** (⊠ Roggeslootweg 3, De Cocksdorp, ☎ 0222/316–539), with a 9-hole links course and a 9-hole practice course.

KAYAKING

Sea and surf excursions and supervised training courses are offered by **Zeekanocentrum Texel** (⊠ Lijnbaan 37, Den Burg,

☏ 0222/315–066) or **SeaMount Tracks** (✉ Rommelpot 19, Den Hoorn, ☏ 0222/319–393), who offer weeklong certificate courses.

PARACHUTING

Paracentrum Texel (✉ Vliegveld Texel, ☏ 0222/311–464) offers supervised training and jumps.

Side Trips A to Z

Arriving and Departing

BY BUS

It's best to take a bus or car to **Aalsmeer,** since the train will take you only as far as Schiphol Airport, where you'll need to transfer to a bus. You can take the NZH Bus 172 from the stop opposite American Hotel near Amsterdam's Leidseplein, or take Bus 171 or 172 from Centraal Station.

BY CAR

To reach **Aalsmeer** by car, take the A4 highway from Amsterdam, pass the Schiphol Airport, and get off at the next exit. **Keukenhof** is to the west of Aalsmeer, off the Lisse exit on A4. To get to the **Zaanse Schans,** you need to navigate the most confusing part of the country's road system, Amsterdam's A10 ring road, from which you take the exit for A8 toward Zaandam. Take the Zaandam exit, then follow local signs. **Hoorn** is north of Amsterdam just off E22/A7. To reach **Enkhuizen** take the Hoorn exit from E22/A7 and continue eastward on N302. To reach **Texel,** travel north from Amsterdam on N203, N9, and N250 to the port of Den Helder.

BY FERRY

The hourly ferry to the island of Texel runs from 6 AM to 9 PM daily in summer. For more detailed **ferry information** call ☏ 0222/369–600. The **TelekomTaxi** (☏ 322–211, local calls only) minibus service takes you from the ferry terminal to your lodgings anywhere on the island of Texel, and picks you up for the return journey if you call an hour ahead. Buy your taxi tickets in advance (Fl 7 per ride) at the ferry ticket office in Den Helder.

To get to **Keukenhof** by train, take the Keukenhof Express train from Amsterdam via Lovers Rail. For more rail information, call 020/557–7666. **Koog-Zaandijk** is the station nearest to Zaanse Schans, on the local line from Amsterdam to Alkmaar. The village can be reached on foot in a few minutes. **Local trains** operate once an hour direct from Amsterdam to Hoorn and Enkhuizen. **Intercity trains** run direct to Den Helder every hour, with connecting buses to the ferry terminal. The **Waddenbiljet** all-inclusive return ticket, the easiest and most economical method for getting to Texel, includes bus services on the island itself. For **national train information** call ☎ 0900/9292 (75¢ per minute).

Contacts and Resources

Contact the local or regional VVV tourist offices (☞ Visitor Information, *below,* and in the Essential Information section) for information about guided group tours and qualified guides.

kantoor Aalsmeer ✉ Drie Kolommenplein 1, 1431 LA, Aalsmeer, ☎ 0297/325–374, FAX 0297/354–255).**VVV Noord Holland** (✉ Oranjekade 41, 2011 VD, Haarlem, ☎ 023/531–9413). **VVV Texel** (✉ Emmalaan 66, 1790 AA, Den Burg, ☎ 0222/314–741, FAX 0222/310–054). **VVV West-Friesland** (✉ Veemarkt 4, 1621 JC, Hoorn, ☎ 0900/ 403–1055, 75¢ per minute; FAX 0229/215–023). **VVV Zaan-streek/Waterland** (✉ Gedempte Gracht 76, 1506 CJ, Zaandam, ☎ 075/616–2221, FAX 075/670–5381).

AMSTERDAM AT A GLANCE: A CHRONOLOGY

1000   According to legend, Amsterdam is discovered by two Frisian fishermen looking for a place to moor their boat in the marshes.

1270   The Amstel River is dammed just south of the present-day Dam.

1275   Count Floris V of Holland bestows the first charter on the settlement of Amstelledamme.

circa 1300   Amsterdam receives city status. The Bishop of Utrecht takes over the city.

1306   Construction begins on Amsterdam's oldest church, the Oude Kerk.

1345   The Miracle of the Holy Sacrament transforms Amsterdam into a pilgrimage center, after an ailing man regurgitates a communion wafer during the last rites. The wafer is tossed into a fire, but miraculously remains intact and the man recovers.

1369   Amsterdam joins the Hanseatic League.

1452   The second of two great fires sweeps the city, destroying nearly all its wooden houses. A law is passed prohibiting the use of wood for the walls of buildings.

1481   The city's fortifications are extended along the Singel, the Kloveniersburgwal, and the Gelderskade.

1489   The insignia of Maximilian I, Archduke of Austria and future Holy Roman Emperor, is included in the city's coat of arms.

1517   The Protestant Reformation occurs in Germany; Lutheran and Calvinist ideas gradually spread to Amsterdam.

1568   The city joins the Dutch Revolt against King Philip II of Spain, Catholic head of the Habsburg Empire and ruler of the Netherlands. The uprising is led by the exiled William of Orange (William I the Silent), and marks the start of the war with Spain, which evolves into the Thirty Years War.

1578 William of Orange gains control of Amsterdam. The Calvinists expel all Catholic leaders from the city.

1589 After the fall of Antwerp to the Spanish, persecuted Protestants and Jews flee to Amsterdam, bringing with them their professional skills and wealth. Banking and ship building flourish, and Amsterdam becomes the hub of the diamond industry.

1602 The Dutch East India Company is established. Transporting silk and spices from the Orient to Amsterdam, the company brings great prosperity. Amsterdam becomes one of the most important trading ports in the world and enters a Golden Age of artistic and cultural activity.

1612 Rapid population growth and increasing wealth lead to the design and construction of concentric rings of canals (including the Herengracht, Keizersgracht, and Prinsengracht) by architect Hendrik de Keyser.

1632 The University of Amsterdam is founded as an academy.

1648 The Thirty Years War ends. Jacob van Campen starts to construct City Hall on the Dam.

1652–54 Wars with England for maritime supremacy begin. Amsterdam's fortunes decline, as England dominates sea routes and commerce stagnates.

1795 The crash of the Amsterdam Stock Exchange, compounded by further war with the English and Napoleon Bonaparte's blockade of continental European trade, marks the end of the Golden Age.

1799 The Dutch East India Company dissolves.

1806 City Hall is taken over by Napoleon's brother, Louis Bonaparte, for use as his Royal Palace.

1814 Following Napoleon's defeat, Prince William VI of Orange seizes power in Amsterdam. He is declared Sovereign Ruler William I of the Netherlands and is invested in the Nieuwe Kerk on March 30th.

1876 The 15-mile-long (27-km-long) North Sea Canal is opened. It connects the former Zuiderzee, the northernmost outlet for the Rhine, directly to the North Sea. The canal brings new prosperity to Amsterdam.

1880 The Free University is established.

1928 The Olympics are held in the city.

1940 On May 15th, Nazi troops occupy Amsterdam.

1941 Amsterdammers declare a spontaneous general strike in protest against Nazi persecution of the city's Jewish population. By the end of the war, most of the Jewish community is exterminated.

1944 While writing her famous diary, Anne Frank is discovered in the Frank family's hiding place on the Prinsengracht and is sent along with the rest of her family to a concentration camp.

1945 On May 7th, the city is liberated by Canadian troops.

1952 The Amsterdam-Rhine Canal opens.

1980 The investiture of Queen Beatrix at the Nieuwe Kerk leads to social uproar and rioting because of the ceremony's waste of state funds.

1986 Amsterdam celebrates its 400th anniversary as a diamond center.

1988 The Stopera complex, designed by Wilhelm Holzbauer, is officially opened. It incorporates the new City Hall and the Music Theater, home to the national opera and ballet companies.

1997 UNESCO places Old Amsterdam on the World Heritage List. A total of 6,936 buildings dating from before 1800 are on the list of state monuments. The City Council decides to reclaim six islands from the IJmeer, creating an artifical archipelago for 18,000 dwellings.

1998 The former President of the Amsterdam-based Dutch National Bank, Willem Duisenburg, is appointed as the first President of the European Central Bank in Frankfurt.

INDEX

✗ = restaurant, ⌂ = hotel

NOTES

NOTES

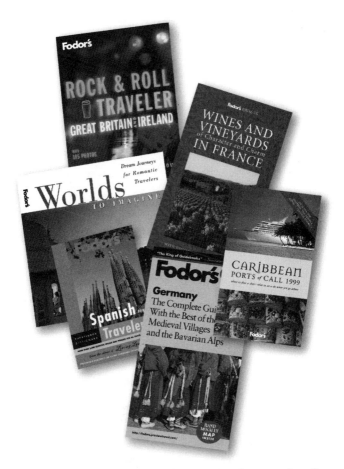

Looking for a different kind of vacation?

Fodor's makes it easy with a full line of international guide-books to suit a variety of interests—from adventure to romance to language help.

At bookstores everywhere.
www.fodors.com

Fodor's Travel Publications

Available at bookstores everywhere. For descriptions of all our titles and a key to Fodor's guidebook series, visit www.fodors.com/books

Gold Guides

U.S.

Alaska
Arizona
Boston
California
Cape Cod,
Martha's Vineyard,
Nantucket
The Carolinas &
Georgia
Chicago
Colorado

Florida
Hawai'i
Las Vegas, Reno,
Tahoe
Los Angeles
Maine, Vermont,
New Hampshire
Maui & Lāna'i
Miami & the Keys
New England
New Orleans

New York City
Oregon
Pacific North
Coast
Philadelphia & the
Pennsylvania
Dutch Country
The Rockies
San Diego
San Francisco

Santa Fe, Taos,
Albuquerque
Seattle &
Vancouver
The South
U.S. & British
Virgin Islands
USA
Virginia &
Maryland
Washington, D.C.

Foreign

Australia
Austria
The Bahamas
Belize &
Guatemala
Bermuda
Canada
Cancún, Cozumel,
Yucatán Peninsula
Caribbean
China
Costa Rica
Cuba
The Czech
Republic &
Slovakia
Denmark

Eastern &
Central Europe
Europe
Florence, Tuscany
& Umbria
France
Germany
Great Britain
Greece
Hong Kong
India
Ireland
Israel
Italy
Japan
London

Madrid &
Barcelona
Mexico
Montréal &
Québec City
Moscow,
St. Petersburg,
Kiev
The Netherlands,
Belgium &
Luxembourg
New Zealand
Norway
Nova Scotia, New
Brunswick, Prince
Edward Island
Paris
Portugal

Provence &
the Riviera
Scandinavia
Scotland
Singapore
South Africa
South America
Southeast Asia
Spain
Sweden
Switzerland
Thailand
Toronto
Turkey
Vienna & the
Danube Valley
Vietnam

Special-Interest Guides

Adventures to
Imagine
Alaska Ports of Call
Ballpark Vacations
The Best Cruises
Caribbean Ports
of Call
The Complete
Guide to America's
National Parks
Europe Ports of Call
Family Adventures
Fodor's Gay Guide
to the USA

Fodor's How to Pack
Great American
Learning Vacations
Great American
Sports & Adventure
Vacations
Great American
Vacations
Great American
Vacations
for Travelers
with Disabilities
Halliday's
New Orleans
Food Explorer

Healthy Escapes
Kodak Guide to
Shooting Great
Travel Pictures
National Parks
and Seashores
of the East
National Parks of
the West
Nights to Imagine
Orlando Like a Pro
Rock & Roll
Traveler Great
Britain and Ireland

Rock & Roll
Traveler USA
Sunday in San
Francisco
Walt Disney
World for Adults
Weekends in
New York
Wendy Perrin's
Secrets Every
Smart Traveler
Should Know
Worlds to Imagine

Fodor's Special Series

Fodor's Best Bed & Breakfasts
America
California
The Mid-Atlantic
New England
The Pacific Northwest
The South
The Southwest
The Upper Great Lakes

Compass American Guides
Alaska
Arizona
Boston
Chicago
Coastal California
Colorado
Florida
Hawai'i
Hollywood
Idaho
Las Vegas
Maine
Manhattan
Minnesota
Montana
New Mexico
New Orleans
Oregon
Pacific Northwest
San Francisco
Santa Fe
South Carolina
South Dakota
Southwest
Texas
Underwater Wonders of the National Parks
Utah
Virginia
Washington
Wine Country
Wisconsin
Wyoming

Citypacks
Amsterdam
Atlanta
Berlin
Boston
Chicago
Florence
Hong Kong
London
Los Angeles
Miami
Montréal
New York City
Paris
Prague
Rome

San Francisco
Sydney
Tokyo
Toronto
Venice
Washington, D.C.

Exploring Guides
Australia
Boston & New England
Britain
California
Canada
Caribbean
China
Costa Rica
Cuba
Egypt
Florence & Tuscany
Florida
France
Germany
Greek Islands
Hawai'i
India
Ireland
Israel
Italy
Japan
London
Mexico
Moscow & St. Petersburg
New York City
Paris
Portugal
Prague
Provence
Rome
San Francisco
Scotland
Singapore & Malaysia
South Africa
Spain
Thailand
Turkey
Venice
Vietnam

Flashmaps
Boston
New York
San Francisco
Washington, D.C.

Fodor's Cityguides
Boston
New York
San Francisco

Fodor's Gay Guides
Amsterdam
Los Angeles & Southern California

New York City
Pacific Northwest
San Francisco and the Bay Area
South Florida
USA

Karen Brown Guides
Austria
California
England B&Bs
England, Wales & Scotland
France B&Bs
France Inns
Germany
Ireland
Italy B&Bs
Italy Inns
Portugal
Spain
Switzerland

Languages for Travelers (Cassette & Phrasebook)
French
German
Italian
Spanish

Mobil Travel Guides
America's Best Hotels & Restaurants
Arizona
California and the West
Florida
Great Lakes
Major Cities
Mid-Atlantic
Northeast
Northwest and Great Plains
Southeast
Southern California
Southwest and South Central

Pocket Guides
Acapulco
Aruba
Atlanta
Barbados
Beijing
Berlin
Budapest
Dublin
Honolulu
Jamaica
London
Mexico City
New York City
Paris

Prague
Puerto Rico
Rome
San Francisco
Savannah & Charleston
Shanghai
Sydney
Washington, D.C.

Rivages Guides
Bed and Breakfasts of Character and Charm in France
Hotels and Country Inns of Character and Charm in France
Hotels and Country Inns of Character and Charm in Italy
Hotels of Character and Charm in Paris
Hotels of Character and Charm in Portugal
Hotels of Character and Charm in Spain
Wines & Vineyards of Character and Charm in France

Short Escapes
Britain
France
Near New York City
New England

Fodor's Sports
Golf Digest's Places to Play (USA)
Golf Digest's Places to Play in the Southeast
Golf Digest's Places to Play in the Southwest
Skiing USA
USA Today The Complete Four Sport Stadium Guide

Fodor's upCLOSE Guides
California
Europe
France
Great Britain
Ireland
Italy
London
Los Angeles
Mexico
New York City
Paris
San Francisco

WHEREVER YOU TRAVEL, *H*ELP IS NEVER FAR AWAY.

From planning your trip to providing travel assistance along the way, American Express® Travel Service Offices are always there to help you do more.

Amsterdam

American Express Travel Service
Van Baerlestraat 39
(31) (20) 6738550

American Express Travel Service
Damrak 66
(31) (20) 5048777

do more

Travel

www.americanexpress.com/travel